PERGAMON INTERNATIONAL LIBRARY
of Science, Technology, Engineering and Social Studies
The 1000-volume original paperback library in aid of education, industrial training and the enjoyment of leisure
Publisher: Robert Maxwell, M.C.

WHY HAS DEVELOPMENT NEGLECTED RURAL WOMEN?

A Review of the South Asian Literature

GW00722404

THE PERGAMON TEXTBOOK INSPECTION COPY SERVICE

An inspection copy of any book published in the Pergamon International Library will gladly be sent to academic staff without obligation for their consideration for course adoption or recommendation. Copies may be retained for a period of 60 days from receipt and returned if not suitable. When a particular title is adopted or recommended for adoption for class use and the recommendation results in a sale of 12 or more copies, the inspection copy may be retained with our compliments. The Publishers will be pleased to receive suggestions for revised editions and new titles to be published in this important International Library.

Other Titles of Interest

BALASSA, B.
Policy Reform in Developing Countries

BHALLA, A.
Towards Global Action for Appropriate Technology

CLARKE, J.
Population Geography and the Developing Countries

ECKHOLM, E.
Losing Ground: Environmental Stress and World Food Prospects

EPSTEIN, T. S. & JACKSON, D.
The Feasibility of Fertility Planning

FITZGERALD, R.
Human Needs and Politics
What It Means To Be Human

JOLLY, R.
Disarmament and World Development

MENON, B.
Global Dialogue: The New International Economic Order

PECCEI, A.
The Human Quality

SINHA, R. & DRABEK, A.
The World Food Problem: Consensus and Conflict

TÉVOÉDJRÈ, A.
Poverty: Wealth of Mankind

TICKELL, C.
Climatic Change and World Affairs

WENK, E.
Margins for Survival: Overcoming Political Limits in Steering Technology

WHY HAS DEVELOPMENT NEGLECTED RURAL WOMEN?

A Review of the South Asian Literature

by

NICI NELSON

Senior Tutor on the "Action-oriented Study
of the Role of Women in Rural Development"

PERGAMON PRESS

OXFORD · NEW YORK · TORONTO · SYDNEY · PARIS · FRANKFURT

U.K.	Pergamon Press Ltd., Headington Hill Hall, Oxford OX3 0BW, England
U.S.A.	Pergamon Press Inc., Maxwell House, Fairview Park, Elmsford, New York 10523, U.S.A.
CANADA	Pergamon of Canada, Suite 104, 150 Consumers Road, Willowdale, Ontario M2J 1P9, Canada
AUSTRALIA	Pergamon Press (Aust.) Pty. Ltd., P.O. Box 544, Potts Point, N.S.W. 2011, Australia
FRANCE	Pergamon Press SARL, 24 rue des Ecoles, 75240 Paris, Cedex 05, France
FEDERAL REPUBLIC OF GERMANY	Pergamon Press GmbH, 6242 Kronberg-Taunus, Pferdstrasse 1, Federal Republic of Germany

First edition 1979

British Library Cataloguing in Publication Data

Nelson, Nici
Why has development neglected rural women?
(Pergamon international library).
1. Women - South Asia - Social conditions -
Bibliography 2. South Asia - Rural conditions -
Bibliography 3. South Asia - Economic conditions -
Bibliography 4. Women - Indonesia - Social
conditions - Bibliography 5. Indonesia - Rural
conditions - Bibliography 6. Indonesia -
Economic conditions - Bibliography
I. Title
016.30141′2′0954   Z7964.S   79-40235
ISBN 0-08-023377-5 hardcover
ISBN 0-08-023376-7 flexicover

In order to make this volume available as economically and as rapidly as possible the author's typescript has been reproduced in its original form. This method unfortunately has its typographical limitations but it is hoped that they in no way distract the reader.

Printed and bound at William Clowes & Sons Limited Beccles and London

This book is the first volume in a new series:
WOMEN IN DEVELOPMENT

Editors: T. Scarlett Epstein and F. P. F. Senaratne, School of African and
Asian Studies, University of Sussex, U.K.

WOMEN IN DEVELOPMENT is the result of the "Action-oriented Study of
the Role of Women in Rural Development", a research project directed by
the editors of this series.
This new and imaginative series is concerned with the world-wide
movements for economic development and female emancipation, with
particular emphasis on the role of women in changing rural societies. Books
planned for the series will review existing research and literature, report on
the problems and successes of current research projects, highlight the main
research lacunae, and outline recommendations for the future role of women
in rural societies.

About the Author

NELSON, NICI. Nici Nelson is a social anthropologist. Her field
experience has been in East Africa where she carried
out research on rural-urban women migrants. The research for this review was carried out in the context
of the "Action-oriented Study of the Role of Women in
Rural Development" directed by T. Scarlett Epstein.
The bibliography so compiled has been utilised by 12
South Asian researchers currently fulfilling their
academic, pre-field training at the University of
Sussex, prior to their starting micro-studies in their
respective countries of origin in the summer of 1978.
They will focus on rural women's economic roles in four
South Asian countries and Indonesia, which hopefully
will help to fill many of the gaps in our knowledge.

Contents

Contents

Chapter I

A Review with a Difference[1]

Introduction

This is a review of the literature available on the role of
women in rural development in South Asia. It is a review with
a difference. Many such exercises are objective surveys of the

[1]The author would like gratefully to acknowledge the grant from
the Rockefeller Foundation without which this research would not
have been possible. Susan Almy gave support and helpful comments.
Needless to say I accept full responsibility for the ideas and
opinions expressed in this review.

I would like to express my gratitude to the many people who gave
their time and effort to assist in compiling the information for
this review. Both Sandra Zeidenstein and Ingrid Palmer kindly
read this paper in an initial draft form and made many useful
suggestions.

All the participants of a Study Seminar on the Role of Women in
Rural Development held in 1977 at the Institute of Development
Studies, the University of Sussex, generously shared their insights and knowledge on the subject with me, especially the two
co-directors, Vina Majumdar and Devaki Jain. Both Tahmina Aziz
and Nancy Dore kindly assisted in my library search at the Institute of Development Studies. Kate Young, Anne Whitehead and
other members of the IDS "Subordination of Women Project" have
contributed numerous insights into the problems inherent in
theorising about women. Rosemary Watts and Mariette Grange were
consistently supportive and patient in helping me prepare this
manuscript for publication.

Special thanks are due to T. Scarlett Epstein. She initially
conceived the project, was a source of inspiration and motivation during my research, and an invaluable critic of the paper
in draft form.

literature on a given subject, which summarize the data available and critically describe the theoretical positions adopted
by various researchers. This review does not claim to take an
objective stance. It has an axe to grind.

What is that axe? It is simply this: too little attention has
been given by researchers and administrators or planners to
women and the roles they play in rural society in the process
of change. The data that exists is piecemeal and difficult to
put together in any meaningful comparative fashion. Due to this
paucity of data, it is impossible to make a substantive summary
of research already done. Instead, the purpose of this review
is to convince those researchers interested in rural women or
in rural development to widen the scope of their concern to in-
vestigate the roles women currently have, and should have in
the future, in the process of rural development taking place in
South Asia, as in other parts of the Third World. Women must
be integrated into the process of rural development not only
because simple justice demands that it be done, but also because
excluding women means under-utilizing a high potential resource,
and this can eventually have adverse effects on the economic
growth rate. Research is necessary to convince planners and
administrators that the potential of women is at the moment
largely untapped by rural development projects.

In this review I start with a definition of what I understand
development to be and the reasons for considering the role of
women in development. I then discuss the categories of sources
that are available which contain data on women in rural development, and some of the reasons why this topic has not received
adequate attention by researchers. In Chapter II I review the
extant literature on women's roles in rural life and economy,
giving credit to the rudimentary research that has already been
done. It must be emphasised that the works cited here are assessed merely on the basis of whether or not they contribute
significantly to our understanding of rural women's lives (especially their economic and decision making roles) or whether they
would be useful in a more practical sense to planners or administrators interested in integrating women into rural development
processes. Obviously there are other goals for researchers and
social analysts, equally admirable. However, these other goals
are not within the scope and interest of the present manuscript.

In Chapter III I assess in some detail how much we presently
know about rural women, and why, how and with what impact women
do or do not participate in development. In the penultimate

chapter I recommend general areas or both theoretical and action-oriented research for consideration in the future by individual researchers and development agencies. In the concluding
chapter I say a few words about appropriate methodology. A bibliography is appended; most, though not all the sources, are
referred to in the body of the article. The sources in the bibliography all include data on, or theoretical analysis of, women,
particularly rural women; most of them do not refer directly to
development issues. Sources dealing with areas other than South
Asia are included only where relevant. Naturally this bibliography does not claim to be exhaustive. Limited time and difficulty of access to unpublished work available only in South Asia
must perforce prevent it from being so.

It is hoped that this review will point the way to future priorities in field studies and encourage new research as well as the
publication of already completed work.

The meaning of development

Development is a concept that can be said to have itself 'devel-
oped' in the last 25 years since it first became an international
concern.

In the early years developers concentrated on increasing the
Gross National Product (GNP). This was a simple and easily
quantifiable variable which appealed to political leaders and
economists alike. It was assumed that there would be a trickle-
down effect from this increased national income. However, disappointingly, if predictably through hindsight, this did not
happen to any notable extent. Since the 1950's, GNP did increase
in many countries throughout the Third World; however, more
equitable distribution did not equalise the character and con-
sequences of development within countries with respect to the
benefits of development and to the areas and categories of the
population affected. "Economic and social benefits have been
limited to higher income groups or to urban populations. Not
only have the benefits not been equally distributed, but there
has recently emerged the concept of 'disbenefits' in which, in
some areas, development has actually worsened economic and social conditions" (United Nations Research Institute for Social
Development 1977 a: 1). For example, in India, Dandekar and
Rath (quoted in Singer, 1973: 43) have shown that the lowest
10% have suffered a decline, both absolutely as well as relatively. Since then, there has been a shift to a concern with

overall social objectives such as the quality of life and the
more equal distribution of the resources of a society. Dag
Hammerskold's *Report on Development and International Co-operation* (Quoted in Dey, 1975: viii) stated grandiloquently that
"Development is a whole. Its ecological, cultural, social, economic institutional and political dimensions" must be understood
and interrelated. It must be an endogenous and self reliant
process in harmony with the environment and dedicated to the
eradication of poverty. Similarly Seers has set out a model of
development which includes the reduction of poverty; the increase
of employment; equality of distribution and opportunity; as well
as an overall category of general rights such as freedom of
speech, citizenship and adequate education (1974).

A number of writers on development have expressed concern that
target populations should participate equally in the development
process: in other words, that they should have self-determina-
tion in the decisions concerning their own welfare and the management of their own economic affairs. In addition it is felt
that development should be integrated and not of the type which
benefits one sector and adversely affects another. To these
ends it must be emphasised that rural development is much more
than an economic or technological process. It is equally a social process that entails a rural transformation (Mbithi, 1972).
New technology, and efforts to increase per capita output and
food production as well as improve rural infrastructure must be
integrated into an on-going socio-cultural process. Only then
can equitable distribution of income and reduction of regional
inequalities and rural-urban migration be reduced. This is the
definition of development to which I adhere.

Why consider the role of women in development?

Recently it has become fashionable to talk about a programme
for Integrated Rural Development. This has led to a realisation, especially since International Women's Year, that special
attention must be paid to the role of women in the development
process. The reason for this is that "women's crucial role in
the development process has generally been neglected and over-
looked" (Olin, forthcoming: 1). In addition women have been
one of the sectors that have been adversely affected by technological and sociological changes brought about by the development process. A number of articulate writers have pointed out
the ways in which women have unequal status in rural areas of
developing countries (Boserup, 1970; Germain, 1975, 1976; Dey,

1975; Olin, forthcoming; Palmern, 1975; Zeidenstein, 1973).
Many U.N. agencies have spoken out on the need for intensified
action to promote equality between men and women and "to ensure
the full integration of women in the total development effort"
(U.N. Economic Commission for Africa, 1975). It is perceived
that the development efforts of the recent past have ignored
the ways in which women's lives and roles have been affected by
conditions of changing technology (ILO, 1975). Women have
been viewed as passive or neutral factors in the socio-economic
and technological transformations being implemented by funding
agencies, economists, planners and administrators. One of the
many results has been that women have not benefited from the
education and training programmes that have in the past taught
new skills to men. A glance at the comparative male-female
literacy rates in most countries reveals this disparity. Technological development has either largely ignored the areas of
life which are women's work (e.g. water fetching, fuel provision
for the household, food processing, food storage) or has usurped
important women's roles, such as craft production, without providing them with any alternative productive functions. Extension
workers often contact the male heads of household exclusively.
Where efforts have been made to operate women's programmes, they
are usually run on a minute budget and are often the first to
be cut when funds are short (Dey, 1975: xi). Recent rethinking
in U.N. agencies has begun to change the emphasis. "Basic
Needs Programmes" are now considered to be the most important
emphasis for such agencies as ILO, UNICEF and others. Since
women are the prime users of basic needs, these programmes are
often directed towards women. Many people are convinced that
women will always convert their resources into helping to meet
basic needs (Palmer, 1975). Other experts have called for the
integration of women in programmes that are not specifically
women-oriented.

Women's role in development is obviously not a simple one; it
relates to a complete range of socio-economic activities. Women
are not only users of basic services, bearers and socialisers
of children, and keepers of the home; where they are under-
employed or inefficient and overworked, they also represent a
productive potential which is not being tapped. Women form half
the population and the development of a country cannot be realised if half the people lag behind. "How can the economic,
social and cultural development of the country be realised where
half of its population (women) is in such great dependency on
the other half" (Nowiki, 1973: 3). Not only does the failure
to include them in the development process run counter to the

true spirit of development but it invariably hinders the process itself. Individual development programmes which do not take into account the co-operation and participation of women may be slowed down and made less effective than they could have been had these aspects been considered. Development planning pro- grammes in agriculture, education, health and nutrition will be most directly affected by ignoring women in the planning process, but in the long run and in varying degrees most programmes deal- ing with commerce, finance and industry will also be affected (Olin, 1977).

Part of the problem in South Asia, as elsewhere in the Third World (see Palla, 1976), has been ignorance at the highest level of government and administration of the participation of women in the rural economy. Hence there is a need for studies of the economic position of women in different societies in order that rural development strategies may be devised and implemented which can bring about equality between the sexes and improve the quality of rural life.

Data sources

In the social sciences in general, and in development studies in particular, there has been very little research done on women. The feminist revolution of the seventies and the impact of Inter- national Women's Year has heralded a change, and the imbalance is in the process of being rectified. Pressure groups have been demanding, quite rightly, that the gaps in our knowledge related to women be filled. This has resulted in a changed attitude on the part of grant agencies and publishers towards studies deal- ing with women.

Some of this work in the social sciences has resulted in a fresh look at previous research and experiences. An example of this is *Women of the Forest* (Murphy and Murphy, 1974). This is a reworking of the authors' original research in a South American society which gives a fresh perspective on the women's half of the culture. As Papanek has pointed out, this is an excellent example of how a "focus on women can improve our general com- prehension of societies" (1975: 194). In anthropology much in- teresting work has recently been published. Some of this work contributes to our comprehension of women in a particular society, such as Strathern's *Women in Between* (1972). Some of it attempts to deal with women as a sociological category, for example *Rosaldo and Lamphere* (eds) *Women, Culture and Society*

(1974). On the other hand there is a pitfall inherent in writing about women as a single sex. We must always be aware of making facile assumptions about women being a single category (Wallman, 1976). This biological attribute is necessarily tempered by conditions of class, race, age, profession, wealth, kinship etc.

Many recnetly published books on women are all too often vague, over-generalised, comparative surveys which include little concrete information except for macro-data such as work participation rates or educational statistics. There are a number of historical examinations of the status of women in particular cultures. Many of these were pioneer works, but often they lack depth and theoretical rigour, concentrating on simple indicators of modernization or advancement of women in their particular contexts. Good examples of this style of research are Vreede de Stuers *The Indonesian Woman: Struggles and Achievements,* (1960), Baig's *Women of India* (1958) and Bhasin's *The Position of Women in India* (1972). There is also a number of general analyses of statistical census data. These are interesting within the limits and constraints of such macro-analysis but they can generate hypotheses only of the most general sort. The analysis they offer can be couched only in the grossest terms. Nath (1968 and 1970) and Youssef (1974) have done this type of analysis on Indian and Muslim women.

Except for studies conducted by a handful of anthropologists, very little research has focused specifically on village women. For our purposes much of the work of these anthropologists is of limited value, though it provides insights into some aspects of women's worlds. The problem is that many South Asian anthropologists have been interested in ritual life and kinship or public sector matters such as caste or village politics. As a result there is more known about variations in style and cultural background of purdah, the ideology of women's position in society, marriage ritual and women's roles in the family than about women's work in villages and what they supply in the way of goods and services. In addition, anthropologists are notoriously disinclined to include hard statistics, especially those relating to economic activities and work allocation schedules. Epstein's groundbreaking study of villages in South India (1962) included household budgets and other carefully compiled village level economic data (though little general information on women). However only a few scholars followed her lead. In 1970 Billings complained that "female farm labour which is of vital importance to the rural economic structure has received scant attention in

economic studies" (1970: 169). That plaint still remains un-
answered.

To put it bluntly, most social scientists who have worked on
women in South Asia have concentrated on elite, urban women in
the modern sector. Studies dealing with rural women in general
or women in rural development in particular are few and far
between (as will be shown below) and these are often pioneer
efforts. Much work remains to be done.

There are four possible categories of sources of information on
rural women of South Asia. In my review of the literature on
South Asia I consulted (i) village studies, either anthropological or agro-economic surveys, (ii) development studies, (iii)
women's studies, (iv) women in rural development studies. In
what follows I briefly assess the type and quality of data available in each of these categories. It is necessary to mention
here why I have not included Family Planning Studies (which are
numerous) as a separate category. After an overview of this
type of data, I concluded that the focus on the knowledge and
practice of family planning was too narrow to be generally useful for a wider view of rural women. The few examples I have
cited are included within the sphere of women's studies.

Village studies are of two types: first, there are anthropological studies based on long term residence in a village which
are conducted by researchers (usually anthropologists) who em-
ploy the technique of participant observation to gather their
data. There are many classic works done in South Asia, though
most have been done in India. These are too numerous to mention. Though they give fascinating pictures of village life,
these studies have two drawbacks concerning data on women. The
first is that too few include statistical data; and the second
is that most of them do not deal in any substantive detail with
women. In most classic anthropological studies done in South
Asia, women as a topic are dealt with only in the chapter related to marriage and family life. Often, insufficient data is
collected on women's economic participation, and only tantalizing glimpses into the role of women in the family management processes are given. There are exceptions; and these are noted in
the next chapter.

Secondly there are agro-economic surveys which have been carried
out by agricultural colleges and institutes on the Sub-continent.
These are usually massive surveys organised on sociological

lines, presenting reams and reams of statistical tables with
little or no analysis to tie them together. They vary in the
amount of attention they pay to the female residents of the
villages they study. Some do not even include such elementary
data as the work participation rates of women inhabitants. Valuable snippets of statistical information on women can be dug out
of these studies, but it would entail a great investment of
time.

Development studies have proliferated as development processes
have accelerated; there have been innumerable studies on rural
development in general or particular projects past and future.
Experts in High Yield Seed Varieties, tractors, irrigation, co-
operatives, population and poultry have flooded South Asia to
write recommendations, reports, proposals, assessments and pre-
dictions. Reading most of these reports could give one the impression that whole regions of South Asia are inhabited solely
by men. Few researchers seem to be aware of the existence of
women except as dependents in the households of male farmers
who have to be included in the calculation of the dependency
ratio. In certain areas, where women of certain categories
draw themselves to the notice of these "experts" by working in
the field, they have been noted as undifferentiated categories
of unpaid family labour, or the lowest group of agricultural
labourers. Again there are few, lamentably few, studies which
have widened their scope to include a consideration of the effects of new projects and technology on the position of women.
An exception which springs to mind is Chambers' *Mwea* (1973), a
description of a rice irrigation settlement scheme in Kenya,
which includes an excellent chapter by Hanger dealing with the
position of women in the scheme, and its effects on the household economy.

Women's studies have become increasingly in vogue since International Women's year. Publishers are eager to cater to the
new interest in women. Many countries have set up Women's
Bureaux to encourage researchers. Studies have varied enormously in quality. There has been a paucity of hard comparable
data or systematic theoretical analysis useful to those interested in altering the condition of rural women. As already mentioned, many of the studies done in South Asia have concentrated
on urban women, or women in the formal economy and have usually
dealt with their attitudes and motivation to work, family situation and child raising. Rural women and their position in the

development process have, for reasons that are stated below,
been largely ignored. One of the difficulties is that few
women writing on women (and it is notable how few men have done
so) are economists with the skills necessary to deal with women's
economic roles

Studies on the role of women in rural development are few and
far between. Ever since Boserup's invaluable pioneer study,
(1970) some scholars have accepted that women play no small part
in economic development processes. Gradually this realisation
has begun to percolate through to development agencies. The
Percy Amendment, which stipulates that all United States' aid-
funded programmes must include a consideration of women, is a
case in point. Credit must be given to the pioneering village-
based studies that have followed Boserup's survey of the subject
(which is often based on admittedly incomplete and sporadic
data) and these are singled out for comment in the next section.

*Why has so little research been done on women's roles in
rural development?*

It is interesting to speculate on why there is a dearth of research on rural women in the context of development studies. I
would like to set out briefly some possible reasons, most of
which may be obvious.

One problem is that many researchers, planners, and members of
funding agencies (the latter two are important because they help
to shape the research concerns pursued in the field) are men.
Many men have a way of perceiving women as basically peripheral
to any important socio-economic process (unless it be child-
care or family planning which are very obviously the concern of
women). Men have in the past planned for, and researched about,
men. Women have been seen as the dependants of males, and their
proper place has been in the calculation of dependency ratios.
The fact that many of the planners, funding agency officials,
and development "experts" have also been middle-class western
men with particular views on the proper place of women (priva-
tised in male "breadwinner's" homes) can have only contributed
to this perception of women's proper place in the development
process.

Where researchers or planners and agency officials have been
women, they have perhaps hesitated to study women, partly because

they have been trained by male colleagues and thus have absorbed
male biases and partly because they are afraid to be labelled
"feminists", a pejorative label for many in the Third World,
as well as in the West.

There are certain practical problems, which may limit women's
ability to carry out research. Women researchers from countries
in South Asia may have difficulty doing work in villages. These
restrictions have been more important in the past, but it is
possible that, in many areas, for young women to go and live
alone in villages while conducting research may still be unthink-
able. Recently, these restrictions have eased in Sri Lanka and
India to the extent that it is possible for women to do research
in isolated villages without incurring the censure of their
families or the villagers they are studying. The social situation is somewhat less relaxed in parts of Pakistan and Bangladesh. The Islamic religion has a more rigid view about the need
to isolate and protect women, particularly those of child-bearing age.

Finally a number of subtle biases held by both researchers and
developers have contributed to the limited quantity of research
on women and concern for them in rural development programmes.
What are these "biases"? Some are conceptual in nature and some
perceptual. The conceptual problems are the definition of development and the definition of work; and the perceptual difficulty
is the definition of the position of women in the rural economy.

The concept of "Development": The specific concept of development used by researchers, planners and administrators has important repercussions on their attitude to women in the development
process. Development is often taken to mean a move toward the
market situation and/or wage employment. Therefore, it is cash
crops and conventionally "productive" activities that receive
the bulk of attention. Women's roles in the informal productive
system and housework are ignored by these pundits of statistical
data. Such a concept of development has led to concentration
on the male heads of households, because they are the family
members who most frequently participate in the formal market
economy. It also accounts for the undue emphasis on studying
elite, educated, urban, 'modern' women who work in the wage
sector. They are the women who are considered to be contribu-
ting to the country's economy because they earn a wage and are
recorded in the labour participation rates.

The concept of "Work": The conceptual difficulty in defining "work" is closely related to the concept of development. The two cannot be easily separated. Statisticians, planners and scholars have problems in defining and quantifying work. Work which is not formalised is not recorded by conventional research tools. There has been a gross under-enumeration of women in the rural work-forces of South Asia due to confusion and contradictions over what is 'productive work', how to deal with 'housework' and who is a 'worker'. Women's work, (bitty, disorganised, discontinuous and not rewarded in money or mentioned in employers' records) has been ignored. Women's work in the rural economy has been seriously under-estimated and a myth of female dependency has grown up (Germain, 1976: 9). "Women do more than is officially noticed" (Zeidenstein, 1975: 4). Data from macro-studies, census and national sample surveys conflict and fail to reveal many of the complex processes of economic life taking place in the villages. Women's labour participation dropped drastically between the 1961 and the 1971 Indian censuses. As has clearly emerged from a number of sources, this is partially due to changes in definitions of workers rather than in actual alteration in work participation patterns (Masani Mehara's contribution to Bhasin, 1972 and Asian Regional Workshop, 1976). There has been some uncertainty over whether or not this change in work participation rates is due entirely to new definitions. Only intensive village-level research can resolve this confusion. Once again, defining productive workers as those who are paid wages leads researchers to emphasise women who work in the formal sectors. The ultimate result of this conceptual confusion is a tendency to define most rural women as dependants who are peripheral to the development process. Since women do not "work" it is only necessary to educate and modernise the male heads of households in order to bring about developmental changes. Women's work has not been modernised or streamlined and thus remains arduous, time consuming, and less productive compared to the work of men. Experts have worked hard to improve the productivity of men's jobs without a commensurate concern for streamlining the complementary work of women, sometimes with unforeseen results. In some areas of Bangladesh the Green Revolution increased the production of rice to the point that the women of the household could not process the harvest efficiently using their old-fashioned, traditional methods. "When there were large harvests of rice in areas of Mymensingh some farmers were marrying extra wives to save on hired female labour" (Zeidenstien, 1975: 7; see also p. 68).

What is the role of rural women in development?

The major perceptual bias which has caused scholars and planners
alike to ignore rural women is a reflection of their difficulty
in seeing women in social interaction at all. Presvelou (1975)
has spoken about the 'invisibility', both physical and social,
of rural women in many countries. Rural women in South Asia are
perhaps more 'invisible' than women anywhere else in the world,
with the exception of the Middle East and North Africa. The
only South Asian country where this does not apply is Sri Lanka.
Women all over South Asia are physically secluded to a greater
or lesser degree; there are variations related to region, religion, class and age. Some researchers have confessed to never
having had a lengthy conversation with a rural woman: e.g.
Carstairs (1975) in India and Bertocci (1975) in Bangladesh.
The physical seclusion of women is a barrier to researchers,
especially male researchers, and this makes it very difficult
for them to assess accurately women's roles in the social and
economic life of the communities being studied. However, physical invisibility is only part of the problem. Social invisibility also accounts for the scant attention paid to women's work
and women's participation in development. Women are not perceived as relevant to the village market and wage economy. This
is where conceptual biases help to shape the senses of perceptions of local populations as well as of outside researchers.
Women's work is casually dismissed as housework by both local
males and researchers alike. One anthropologist maintains that
Bengali men do not realise how much women do, nor do they appre-
ciate their important role in production (Arens, 1975: 49).
This perception of women as irrelevant to economic pressures has
led planners, when they have given a thought to the condition of
the female half of their "target populations", to assume that
it is enough to consider the male head of the household. There
is evidence that this assumption is fallacious, and the failure
to include women in the development process can have unexpected
negative results (Alamgir, 1977: 67-8). Women may conceivably
act as a conservative force opposing change, both social and
technological (Wolf, 1972; Palmer, 1975). Even the assumption
that the head of the household is male has its dangers, since
there is growing data to show that as many as one third of the
world's household heads may be women (Tinker, 1976).

At the same time developers often think that in order to up-
grade and improve women's position it is sufficient to raise a
family's income. This assumes an automatic 'trickle down' of
benefits from the male head of the family to all its other

members. Women's greatest problems are regarded as merely those
affecting the whole society: the population explosion, lack of
food and jobs etc. It is felt that once these have been dealt
with adequately, then it will be time to show concern for women.
While it is true that an improvement of a family's income is
bound to have *some* positive effect on the lives of that family's
women, it is spurious to assume that if general societal problems
are met and solved, then women will automatically benefit. On
the contrary, as I try to indicate below, the solution of particular problems of increased output can have quite the opposite
result. At the same time, it is not true that showing concern
for the particular needs of women will inhibit the solution of
general poverty problems. Programmes directed towards women
can and do have more general positive effects. For example,
raising the educational levels and economic opportunities for
girls would have positive effects on fertility control goals
(Zeidenstien, 1973: 6).

Chapter II

Literature on Rural Women of the Asian Sub-continent

This chapter examines in detail the published data on the role of women in rural development that is available for each of the four countries of South Asia: Bangladesh, India, Pakistan and Sri Lanka. I concentrate on those studies which I consider worthy of consideration.

Bangladesh

Though Bangladesh is a young and relatively poor country compared to the other three states of South Asia, several high quality pieces of research have been published on rural women and women in development. This concern for rural women and their position has undoubtedly sprung from the war in 1970 and the resultant plight of the widows and raped women (see the National Board of Bangla Women's Rehabilitation Programme, *Women's Work*, 1974). As a result, international agencies such as the Ford Foundation have encouraged a number of scholars to produce short studies focusing on the role of rural women in development.

There are four village studies of high quality which contain much of value on the lives of rural women. McCarthy (1967), Hara (1967), Ahmed (1968) and Arens (1977) have written interesting theses which deal wholly or in part with the lives of rural women. Unfortunately, except for Arens none of them has been published, and they are difficult to obtain in Britain. Ahmed's work, though ostensibly about the peasant family, includes some data on comparative work organization in the family which is related to class status. Hara's study of kinship concentrates on family status, marriage and purdah but does include information on women's life cycles and women's daily work schedules. Aren's book is also not specially about women, but is rather on examinations of rural peasant life; a male-female team carried out the research and there is much data of interest about rural women, though much of it is slightly exaggerated in

15

tone. Unfortunately, I could not read the McCarthy thesis, but
have included it in the bibliography because it is widely quoted
and frequently cited as an excellent pioneer work that deserves
credit.

Much research has been done on development in Bangladesh, even
when it was still East Pakistan. The Comilla district has become a development prototype. An Integrated Rural Development
scheme begun there in 1956, setting up a two-tiered co-operative
system, has been well described in the literature. However, the
participation of women in these co-operatives, which were designed to give credit facilities and training to increase local
production, has been so minimal that Ali, writing in 1975, could
dismiss village women by saying that they "observe purdah and
make little contribution to economic development" (p. 36).
Women's position in the development process is usually covered
by a description of the Comilla Rural Development Programmes
designed for women. For example a long book edited by Stevens
and Bertocci, *Rural Development in Bangladesh and Pakistan*,
(1976) mentions rural women on only two pages out of more than
300 describing the Comilla programme which will teach women "how
to get about with dignity, how to earn small sums of money
through a variety of economic activities convenient to their
household obligations and how to enrich the health and social
life of their families" (1976: 117). This reflects a view that
women's programmes are the frills, the extras, peripheral to
the important central issues of development. Women will learn
how to 'get about' and 'earn small sums'. This emphasis may
be changing if the women's programmes described by Abdullah and
Zeidenstine (1978) are expanded.

As I said before, the war stimulated an interest in and a concern for women in Bangladesh. One of the best and most comprehensive profiles of Bengali women, considering the scarcity of
genuine village level studies available, is Alamgir's *Profile
of Bangladesh Women*, (1977). Unlike so many of the works on
Indian women reviewed in the next section, there is not an undue emphasis on urban, elite women. Rural women are given the
weight they deserve as 90% of Bangladesh women. This study ad-
dresses itself to many important questions: women's work, decision-making, control of resources, credit facilities (use of
and access to), marketing of produce and education. It is hampered by a scarcity of primary data, and raises more questions
than it can answer. Karim's contribution to Barbara Word's
Women in the New Asia, written earlier in 1963, falls into the
trap of considering urban educated women as 'the Bangladeshi

woman'. Jahan's much later work (1975) attempts a more balanced presentation of the political and social status of all Bangladesh women, as does Smock (1977).

However, where the literature is strongest (relative to other South Asian countries) is in the area of rural women in the rural economy and the role of women in development programmes. There are available a number (not many, but one hopes, a sign of more to come) of concerned overviews of women in rural development, as well as several village studies focusing on rural women. Those that are available are not always specifically concerned with development programmes or processes, yet they could be very helpful for development planners and administrators. Germain (1976), Lindenbaum (1974), Kabir (1976), and Zeidenstein (1973, 1976 and 1977), have produced thoughtful summaries of the issues and difficulties facing women in the Bangladesh development process. These are of more use in formulating hypotheses for testing in future research than they are in terms of concrete data and proven hypotheses; however they include concrete data that assess current development programmes specifically tailored for women. Martius Von Harder (1975) and Chen (1977) have both produced interesting quantitative data; the former on the effects of the introduction of High Yielding Varieties of rice on rural women, and the latter on the Food for Work Programme's female clients. These two studies point the way to future research projects. They include grass roots, face to face studies, coupled with a knowledge of economic and technological issues. They provide some of the most specific and testable data and hypotheses concerning women's place in rural development so far available. O'Kelly has recently compiled a list of simple rural technologies available for rural women of Bangladesh (1977). It is a practical guide on technologies for homestead post-harvest activities and for obtaining water; but it would have benefited from some assessment of alternative methods. M. Islam has also produced a practical manual for food preparation (1977): most helpful, though it unfortunately concentrates on relatively high level technology needing too much equipment for poverty-stricken rural women.

Sattar and Ellikson have contributed two fine articles on rural women in *Women for Women* (1975). Their concerns are more general, but the data they have provided on women's work (in the case of Sattar) and on the lack of independent women as women's role models (in Ellikson's study), make their work valuable. Abdullah's *Village Women as I saw Them,* (1974) compiles some basic statistics about women in 20 Comilla villages collected

in the 1960's. It is mainly a descriptive study; the section
on women's work activities is not very informative, though the
sections on marriage and education are more so.

There have been several noteworthy analyses of specific Bangladesh rural development programmes for women. I have already
mentioned Chen's study of the Food for Work Programme (1977).
Abdullah and Zeidenstien are soon to publish a fascinating assessment of the Women's Programme of the Bangladesh Integrated
Rural Development Programme. I was lucky enough to see the
first draft (1978). This study will contribute much to our
knowledge of how a women's programme can be successfully initiated. The sections on the training of the programme staff and
the organisation of the credit schemes directed to village women
are of special interest. Three intensive case studies of different co-operatives yield interesting data and raise important
questions on the formation, composition, organisation and leadership of rural women's co-operatives, including insights into
how members use their loans. This document, thorough and honest
in its appraisal, presents a model of how future assessments of
on-going rural development schemes should be conducted.

McCarthy's examination of the use of loans by female co-operative members provides information on how 70 women out of 1992
I.R.D.P. co-operative members in 7 Thanas of Bangladesh used
the loans they received (1977). In order that future credit
programmes for women can be better directed towards the poorest
members more such studies are needed to provide planners with
feed-back. These case studies clearly indicate the need for
women's income-generating programmes. A UNICEF feasibility
survey was conducted on programmes in Bangladesh currently attempting to give rural women increased income-earning potential.
The report concluded that the various programmes often did not
pay enough attention to marketability of the products (either
in quality or in market demand). Also they do not always reach
the poorest women which they all claim to serve. Again, as an
assessment of on-going programmes, it is an important contribution to our knowledge about the development process and its
effect on women (UNICEF Dacca, 1977).

In Bangladesh a start has been made on research into rural
women and their role in development. It is to be hoped that
the studies cited have laid the foundation for more rigorous
work in the future. The remaining questions still outnumber
the available answers.

India

There have been innumerable village studies carried out by anthropologists both before Independence by British anthropologists
and after Independence by Indian scholars. Most of these studies
contain remarkably little material on women. For instance,
Epstein's study of two South Indian villages (1962) had only
one brief section on women, 4 pages out of a total of 335.
Many anthropologists have been mesmerized by Indian caste or
ritual systems. The studies contianing meaningful data on women
are the exception rather than the rule. The Wiser's *Behind Mud
Walls*, (1963) based on observations made in the 1930's, included
much about women and their role in family decision-making, perhaps because they were a husband and wife team. Dube (1955) includes a chart of village seasonal work broken down by sex.
Bailey has some tantalizing, but incomplete information on women
traders (1957); incomplete in the sense that he was not interested in exploring some of the differences in family management
patterns that this trade within and outside the village might
produce. With depressing regularity women are relegated to the
chapter on marriage rituals or the organization of the family
in its structural sense.

There are, on the other hand, three relatively recent exceptions
to this neglect of rural women by writers of village studies:
Jacobson's *Hidden Faces* (1970), Luschinsky's *Life of Women in
a Village in North India* (1962), and Vreede de Stuer's *Purda:
A Study of Moslem Women's Life in North India* (1968). These
three studies provide valuable insights into many aspects of
village women's lives, even though the authors have been more
interested in marriage rituals, religious rituals and the mechanisms and operation of the institution of purdah. For example
Luschinsky devoted only 64 pages out of nearly 766 to women's
work, while presenting whole chapters on early childhood, infancy,
later childhood, pregnancy, bride in the in-laws' home, and
marriage rituals. However, she does give information on the
differential work patterns of women of different castes and on
women's authority in the household. Jacobson makes an interesting comparison of Hindu and Moslem women in a North Indian
village and the differences in the operation of purdah. She expresses much interest in decision-making power and participation
in family management; though she relates differences in women's
power in these matters to the type of family (nuclear versus
extended) and neglects the caste-class affiliation of women and
their differential work participation as a possible determining
factor. Vreede de Stuers is mainly concerned with purdah of

Moslem women in Hindu India. One regretable fact is that only
Vreede de Stuers' work is published. The other two are unpublished theses, though some of Jacobson's original data can be
found in a symposium, *Many Sisters* (1974). It is greatly to be
regretted that these two penetrating studies, rich in primary
data, are not more easily available.

In the present climate of interest in women, certain anthropologists have been moved to re-examine their original data in order
to write about women. Beteille (1975), Carstairs (1975) and
Madan (1975) are good examples of this reassessment of old data
in the light of new concerns. Unfortunately, none of them are
particularly rigorous or analytical. Srinivas (undated and
1976a) has produced a much more interesting attempt to confront
the problem of women (rural and urban), albeit in a very general
model with little primary data to support it. Hopefully, in the
future, researchers in the rural area, regardless of their concerns and their sex, will be motivated to collect more data on
rural women as well as men. For example, Monica Das Gupta,
doing an Indian village study in 1974 on a more general demographic topic, collected excellent material which has permitted
her to write two very good papers on the women of her village
(1975, 1976). It is to be hoped that this will be the future
trend of village research.

There are innumerable examples of agro-economic surveys which
have been carried out in India by the Census of India as well
as the various agricultural institutes. These studies compile
data on land holding, cropping patterns, and income. The series
of village studies carried out in the '50's and '60's by Bharati
usually mention women in only two or three paragraphs: i.e.
those dealing with agricultural labourers, dependency ratios,
or family labour.

Development studies carried out in India have been largely
blinkered on the topic of rural women and their economic roles.
With few exceptions one can find little relevant information in
these studies. Two exceptions are Dantwale (1975) and B.
Dasgupta *Village Society and Labour Use* (1977). The latter includes data on rural women, especially on time allocation,
though he too makes the point that for South Asia such information is scarce indeed.

There is a tradition in India of concern with the status of
women. This stems from the early interest shown by political
reformers on the subcontinent in matters related specifically

to women. Such issues as widow self-immolation, child marriage
and the forbidding of widows to remarry formed dramatic rally-
ing points for those intellectuals and politicians who were
attempting to oppose British imperialism (Omvedt, 1975: 46).
Ghandi himself was partially responsible for this interest in
the position of women, for he always urged that women should
participate actively in the political campaigns for Independence.
Urban elite women were encouraged to take part in the demonstrations and party politics that preceded the achievement of self-
rule.

This concern for the status of women led to a proliferation of
studies on women by local scholars. However, few of the works
(even the more recent ones) deal in a rigorous and detailed manner with rural women. Of the better known Indian studies on
women in the last 20 years, most have been historical treatments
of the status of women from the time of the Vedas to the role
of women in the Freedom Movement, or general overviews of women's
present social, political and religious status, often without
clarity classifying "women". They often include detailed lists
of the very real legal improvements that have been carried out
in the last 50 years to enhance the status of women.

K. Dasgupta has published an annotated bibliography, *Women on
the Indian Scene*, (1976). This enables a swift assessment to
be made of the emphasis to be found in the output of most scholars writing on Indian women in the last few years. Out of
117 sources of women's participation in the economy of India,
only 8 deal with rural women, a total of 6%. In other sections,
e.g. education, the percentage of books and articles relating
to rural women is as low as 2%.

Three relatively early general books on Indian women are T. A.
Baig (ed) *Women of India* (1958), Neera Desai *Women in Modern
India* (1957) and Sengupta *Women in India* (1964). Baig's book
includes 3 historical studies, 3 political-legal status studies,
9 articles listing elite women's participation in the fine arts,
sports, professions, voluntary services etc. and one article on
tribal women. Desai's book deals almost exclusively with the
historical development of the position of women, with special
emphais on modern political movements. Sengupta is interested
in the political status of women, legal rights, improvements in
education, and rights to work in the modern sector. One page
only is devoted to rural women in a passing reference to a planning commission's design to improve villagers' living standards
by setting up co-operatives that would allow women to market
handicrafts.

However, academic interest in the rural 80% of Indian women has
not increased a great deal with the passage of time. M. Roy's
Bengali Women (1972), C. Hate's *Changing Status of Women* (1969)
and Madan's "Hindu Women at Home" (1975) talk in the most general
terms about women's life cycles. Roy is admittedly interested
only in upper class urban women, while Hate makes no distinction
between rich and poor, urban and rural women. Trivedi (1976)
examines marriage patterns and ideals among educated Jain Bania
girls. Three important symposia on women have come out in the
1970's; Devaiki Jain (ed) *Indian Women* (1975), A. De Souza (ed)
Women in Contemporary India (1975) and B. Nanda (ed) *Indian Women
from Purdah to Modernity* (1976). None of these gives rural
women the weight that their sheer numerical superiority and the
undeniable importance of the rural sector would warrant. In
Jain's book only three articles out of twenty-two deal with rural
women, and one of those is reprinted from Baig's book (1958).
De Souza's symposium includes two in-depth studies of village
women, out of a total of 11 articles, while Nanda's includes
among seven articles only one study of work power and the status
of rural women.

In response to International Women's Year, India appointed a
committee to prepare an extensive report on the status of women
in India. This detailed report, *Toward Equality* (1974), is a
general summary of demographic, legal and statistical data on
women with lengthy sections on the position of women in the
different religious communities and the different types of kinship systems to be found in India. These are interesting theoretical areas that deserve examination; the rural sector, however, is largely neglected. For example, most of the long section on women's work participation deals only with participation in the modern sector. Undoubtedly, primary data was un-
available, and limits of time and financial resources restricted
the organisers.

There are very few studies available which deal with the subject
of women's participation in development. Some articles attempt
a macro-analysis of women's work force participation in India
(Billings, 1970; Gulati, 1975; Nath, 1968, 1970; Reddy, 1975;
P. Sengupta, 1960; Tharmarajakshi, undated), but they suffer
from the limitations of all analyses based on broad, census-
style data. First of all, only certain quantifiable questions
can be adequately dealt with by such methods. Secondly, hypotheses tested against such general data end by being so general
as to be almost useless to planners and administrators who are

interested in framing village level projects. Theoretically, these hypotheses may be of importance, but they should be tested in a micro-level research situation in order to add depth and meaning to sweeping generalisations. To my knowledge, little of this village level testing has as yet been carried out.

There are some exceptions to this trend towards census analysis of the role of women in rural development. Bhatt (1978) has described a project unionising female agricultural workers. Sengupta, in an early work, *Women Workers of India*, (1960) dealt in some sociological detail with women on plantations. D. Jain has done an intensive study of women workers on tea plantations, *Women Workers and Family Planning in the Tea Industry*, (1976) which assesses a family planning programme run by the Tea Industry for women workers. This report gives an insight into the lives, work, socialisation and family organisation of women tea plantation employees. It also examines the creches run by the plantations and the social extension workers who operate in that milieu. *Indian Farming* had a special issue on women (Nov. 1975) which included some substantive articles on agricultural programmes, extension worker services available to women, and the response of women in some regions to new technology. Chakravorty, a contributor to this volume, has also provided a description of rural women's work in Maharashtra which emphasises the largely unappreciated burden of tasks borne by them (1975). Nath has produced two interesting papers based on in-depth village level research in which she has attempted to come to grips with various development issues. In the first, published in 1965, she examines women's work roles and the effects that the so called Green Revolution in the Punjab has had on them. In the second she compares the lives of women of three different castes in three different villages in Rajasthan and the effect that different sexual divisions of labour have had on women's participation in decision making, power within the family, family nutrition and domestic relations.

New research is undoubtedly in the pipeline; we await the results with interest. Devaki Jain at the Institute of Social Studies in New Delhi is currently processing the raw data from an in-depth time disposition study of 125 rural households in six villages in two different Indian states. The objective of the study is to develop concepts and methodology suited to the measurement of female work participation based on an analysis of causal relationships between female activity patterns and the socio-economic setting in which they operate. Vina Mazumdar of the Indian Social Science Research Council is interested in

attempting an intensive, historical analysis of official records
and censuses with a view to establishing a more accurate picture
of women's participation in the non-household economy in the
late 19th and early 20th century.

In conclusion, it would be safe to say that though there is a
great deal of material available on women in India, very little
of that relates to rural areas, and even less to the role of
women in rural development.

Pakistan

The quantity of work dealing with Pakistani women, either directly or indirectly is limited. As elsewhere the quality of
this work varies enormously. Some studies have been produced,
but most are general histories of the socio-legal position of
women or relate to modern sector and elite women. Purdah has
received a large share of the interest by foreign scholars who
have studied Pakistani women, for obvious reasons. The seclusion of women there is very explicit and it has captured the
imagination of many writers on Moslem women.

There are two bibliographies on available studies of Pakistani
women, Helbock (1975) and Mayo (1976). Both of these illustrate
vividly the dearth of data on rural women and their participation in the rural economy. In Mayo's bibliography 157 sources
are listed out of which only 15 are concerned with rural women.
Similarly Helbock's annotated bibliography consists of 35 pages
of sources, of which only one is devoted to rural women. The
conference on "the Role and Status of Women in Pakistan" held
for International Women's Year in Lahore had 57 reading papers:
one dealt specifically and solely with rural women, whilst two
included rural women within their ambit.

There is a surprising absence of village studies done in Pakistan. Why this should be so is difficult to tell, unless that
part of colonial India was regarded as being outside the main-
stream of village research. It must be remembered that Pakistan as Pakistan did not exist until the partition in 1947.
Therefore the area that is now Pakistan was merely on the fringes
of India, which provided the focus of academic interest for
social scientists. Perhaps, as Akbar Ahmed has suggested (personal communication), there were two other factors which made
field work in Pakistan less easy. First the strong Moslem male
bias in society might have contributed to hostile attitudes

towards outsiders investigating village affairs, and secondly
many parts of Pakistan were geographically more isolated and
difficult than India; it is perhaps no accident that the Punjab
plains to the South have monopolised the interest of researchers
in the past. Whatever the reasons, there are few village
studies, except for Elgar (1957, 1960) and Barth (1959). Barth
barely mentions women at all in his model of the strategising
Khans. Elgar however does include a certain amount of data on
women, marriage, women's work and the differences to be found
between landowner and artisan women.

Most of the development literature concerning Pakistan has been
purely technical and economic in scope. Like the commensurate
literature done in India and Bangladesh there is little or no
concern shown for the roles of women in technical and economic
processes.

International Women's Year sparked an interest in women in
Pakistan, as elsewhere. As already mentioned, a national conference was held at Lahore on "The Role and Status of Women in
Pakistan" (1975), and a similar Symposium took place in the
same year at the Pakistan Institute for International Affairs.
Neither of them attached much weight to the problems of rural
women. At the former, most of the delegates concentrated on
historical analysis of legal changes or examinations of the
status of women within the ideology and practice of Islam. At
the conference organised by the Pakistan Institute for International Affairs, many of the delegates displayed remarkable
conservatism, warning against 'Women's Liberation' as being
essentially opposed to the tenets of eastern philosophy, Islamic
religion, and the happiness of the family. The concluding speech
summarises the future of Pakistani women thus:

"The future role of women in Pakistan is therefore, mostly,
though not entirely, inside the home as doting daughters,
winsome wives and moulding mothers rather than outside the
home as careless clerks, wearisome workers, and dancing
damsels . . . In short they should be home-oriented, soft
spoken, modest and yielding. In this manner they can contribute to human happiness by reducing life's tensions and
troubles" (1975: 80).

The writer was obviously thinking in terms of middle-class urban
women, viewing them as the economic dependants and emotional
support of well-off, middle class men. If this is indicative
of attitudes prevailing amongst male politicians, administrators

and academics, Pakistan's leadership is more conservative on
this issue than those of India and Bangladesh. There is no
simple answer as to why this should be so. It may in past be
due to Islam's preoccupation with men rather than women. Perhaps there is a scarcity of highly educated women occupying
political, administrative and academic posts who could serve to
make respectable the issue of increasing women's extra-familial
roles and active participation in development processes.

There have been a few women's studies done by local and foreign
scholars. Three early ones are Honigmann (1957), Ikramullah
(1958) and S. Ahmed (1967) which concentrate mainly on the perception of women, women's nature, and women's role behaviour
(especially within the confines of the institution of purdah).
This concern with the perceptual aspects of women and women's
roles in purdah is also characteristic of the work by Helbock
(1975a), Papanek (1971, 1973) and Pastner (1971, 1974). These
three scholars have contributed much of worth both in terms of
ethnographic detail (for rural Baluchistan in Pastner's case)
and of theoretical analysis of the institution of purdah itself
and the ideology which lies behind it. This is valuable ground
work which needs to be pursued further. Physical seclusion and
the social invisibility of women are interrelated problems which
have to be faced on a theoretical as well as a practical level
by anyone interested in understanding the lives of rural women.
More work must be done in this area, especially in assessing
the strategies of women within the confines of purdah and the
factors which could practically inhibit changes in their socio-
economic activities.

Several family planning studies done in Pakistan yield insights
into rural women's lives, despite the fact that they focus on
relatively limited comparisons of quantifiable variables. Both
Hardee (1975) and Shah (1975) attempt to correlate educational
and economic factors with acceptance of family planning. Gardezi's *The Dai Study* (1969) analyses a programme which attempted
to utilise the expertise of local midwives, and to integrate
them into a family planning and general health and hygiene programme. The philosophy of upgrading the skill of local practi-
tioners and giving them paramedical status has been used successfully in rural China. The Pakistani experiment was not totally
satisfactory, due to its limited training programme. However,
it is an interesting case study of the way in which village
women's skills may be capitalised on, rather than ignored by
planners.

I could locate only six studies concentrating solely on Pakistani rural women and some aspect of development. Two of these are exciting examples of the type of research that is so badly needed: Anwar's and Bilquee's work *The Attitudes, Environment and Activities of Rural Women* (1976) and Saeed's *Rural Women's Participation in Farm Operations* (1966). The former is admittedly only based on two weeks research in a village, but it is perhaps a prototype of future research for other scholars, male and female. It covers a wide range of topics on rural women: education, aspirations for daughters' education; purdah; knowledge, attitudes and use of family planning; daily and annual tasks; and women's skills. This wide-ranging data with an emphasis on economic and farming activities may be useful to rural development planners. However, because the study is based on only a fortnight's work, it is necessarily impressionistic; time allocation data and information on constraints on family labour can only be obtained by intensive research over long periods. Saeed's data on work participation of women is more limited in scope, and she does not state the amount of time she spent in the village. Since she was attempting to establish the correlation between farm work and caste affiliation, her interests are narrower. Again she did not collect any comprehensive data on hours spent on various work tasks.

The remaining studies of women in development are less innovative. Two of them concentrate on the education of rural women (Copping, 197, and Hashimi, 1968) and are merely reviews of programmes already under way, including rhetorical statements on the importance of expanding educational opportunities for girls. However, Hashimi has given a thoughtful, if impressionistic, presentation of the roles and farm management responsibilities fo rural women, concluding with some of the barriers which limit the education of rural women. Anis Ahmed's article on "The Role of Women in Integrated Rural Development Programmes" (1976) gives an uninspired list of the type of activities and training programmes for women offered under the present IRDP approach in Pakistan. He presents little or no assessment of the programmes, beyond maintaining that the main target group of socio-economic and cultural up-lift programmes must be women in order "to bring life and cheer into the dreary lives" of women (op. cit: 33); a goal so general and unspecified as to be meaningless. However, his practical recommendations for programmes, including nurseries to look after trainees' children, women's co-operatives to carry out commercial activities, and interest-free loans provided through government funds are clear-sighted and show a grasp of some of the problems facing rural women.

In conclusion, the available work on Pakistani women in general
and women in the rural sector in particular, has been limited
in scope, quantity and quality.

Sri Lanka

In Sri Lanka there is very little information on women in the
anthropological or development literature and there have been
very few studies carried out on women, whether rural or urban.

There are several standard ethnographies for Sri Lanka: Leach's
Pul Eliya (1961), Pieris's *Sinhalese Social Organisation* (1956),
Obeysekere's *Land Tenure in Village Ceylon* (1967), and Yalman's
Under the Bo Tree (1967). Only the latter contains any extensive data on women. The first three, largely concerned with
kinship and its relationship to land tenure systems, mention
women only in passing while referring to marriage institutions
or female inheritance rights under each of the two possible forms
of marriage (characterised by either uxorilocal or virilocal
residence). Yalman's interests are broader, including a consideration of women and their position in these institutions.
Alexander's (1963) unpublished thesis on a fishing village presents the most considered and systematic data on village women.
Women's economic roles (within and outside the home), their decision-making powers and their position in local systems of kinship and marriage are all examined.

There are also a limited number of ethnographic journal articles
on Sri Lankan villages; e.g. Von Fellenbert (1965); Pieris
(1962, 1965); Ryan (1955); and Siniwardene (1958). Most of
these hardly deal with women at all. Von Fellenberg discusses
women's roles in the context of the division of labour and
makes only a passing reference to the women's leaders who organ-
ise women's mutual assistance groups for weeding and harvesting
(1965: 121). Pieris, in two articles on village development,
dismisses women as a topic with the off-hand statement that
"Women assist in these operations (of slash and burn agriculture)" (1965: 175); such casual treatment of women's contribution to productive work is refuted by Ryan in his article on
a village with a similar agricultural system. Ryan examines the
family division of labour in detail and argues that women have
much, and in some cases all, the responsibility for the slash
and burn agriculture (1955: 154) and contribute all the labour
for the collection of nuts from the forest which is a major
source of cash income for the family (Ibid: 157). He also

mentions women's informal co-operation in harvesting. Siniwardene (1958), in a description of the social structure of a Sinhalese village, presents in a disorganised, non-analytical way, brief information on women's literacy rates (lower than males), work force participation (they constitute 14% of the labour force), leisure activities (gossiping and making mats and bags), eating habits (they eat after the men), status (a woman with a big dowry has more authority in the home), and socialisation (they are supposed to be modest and shy).

Sri Lankan development studies provide little of interest on women and their role in development processes. My perusal of what was available yielded almost nothing. For example, Abeywardena's paper (1977) on improving rice production, though written for a conference on women in rural development, contained no reference to women. Ranasinghe's *Bibliography of Socio-Economic Studies in the Agrarian Sector of Sri Lanka* (1977) lists one source which deals explicitly with women: a group of papers for a UNESCO conference held in New Delhi in 1954.

Women's studies have been correspondingly few and far between. One of the earliest, Siniwardene's contribution to *Women in the New Asia* (1963) is a general description of women and their position in the belief systems of traditional Sri Lanka. Women are defined as seeking the twin ideals of being a good wife and a good mother. They are protected and secure, yet "they were considered inferior to men in all aspects and a constant source of trouble and wickedness" (1963: 151).

The only other sources of Sri Lankan women I could locate were those that concentrated primarily on urban women in formal wage employment and education. Kannangara (1966), in an early summary of women's employment, does include data on women's work participation on tea plantations. Jayaweera (1976) is interested mainly in the formal education of women and is a good source of information on the enrolment of women from primary to University levels. There is a short section at the end on nonformal sector education which relates more directly to rural women; however, little of substance on the subject is presented. Siniwardene's (1974) article on education and employment prospects concludes without originality that both the educational system and the wage sector are dominated by men. The statistics of Castillo (undated) consist of compilation of government census data unilluminated by any analysis.

Two articles by anthropologists, Obeysekere (1963) and Yalman
(1963) are theoretically more interesting. The former deals
with pregnancy cravings among Sinhalese village women and this
necessitates a close examination of how women are locally perceived and the correct roles for them, and the antagonism between
the sexes, which together create "pressing psychological problems for women" (1963, p. 332). Yalman is interested in the
South Asian purity of women and how it fits into the Sinhalese
caste system with its bilateral emphasis; although admittedly
he is more concerned with the operation of the caste system
than with the position of women within it.

There is almost nothing else available on women in rural development. Whether or not material exists in Sri Lanka itself is
impossible to say. All that I could locate in the UK were
several issues of *Economic Review* and Jayaraman (1975). Jaya-
wardena's article (1975) in *Economic Review* on Sri Lankan women
is a very wide-ranging, but superficial, treatment of the subject,
covering everything from work participation statistics to content analysis of school books for sex-role stereotypes. Rural
women are treated primarily in the section on plantations. *Economic Review* (Sept. 1976) also has a special issue on "Women
and Development" — the title is perhaps revealing: the use of
an "and" instead of an "in" may indicate the editor's uncon-
scious feeling that women are basically outside the development
process. This issue has 9 articles, on such topics as family
dominance in agriculture, employment, law, international con-
ventions, community health, cultural structures of discrimination, appropriate technology and women's role in the rural economy. Although rural women are given an appropriate amount of
space in the presentation of the material, most of the data presented is statistical and very general in nature. One of the
more thoughtful of the articles is Goonatelake's which outlines
how discrimination against women is rooted in the economic,
social and cultural structures of Sri Lanka. Unfortunately,
it is too brief to develop the argument properly. Jayaraman
(1975) has, on the other hand, provided us with an intensive
examination of women's lives on tea plantations. More work of
this nature is needed.

A number of female Sri Lankan scholars (including Padmini Abeywardena, Ann Abeywardena and Aruna Dayaratne) have confirmed
my impression that very little has been written on the topic
of women in development. It is for this reason that we await
with interest the results of Perera's current research on women
and development. This research is designed to examine the

influence of development on the lives of rural women with
special emphasis on the grass root experiences of women. It
sets up criteria to assess change, such as the degree of women's
access to resources and their ability to fulfill their needs,
the degree of socio-economic self-reliance and women's active
participation in public life (1977).

Chapter III

What May Have Been Learned So Far

As the tone of this review so far indicates, although there has
been a certain amount written about the effects on rural women
of the socio-cultural changes resulting from new technology
and increasing integration in the world market economy, most
of it remains at the level of assertion without the backing of
concrete data (Bossen, 1975: 588). However, before going into
detail about the type of research that needs to be done in the
future, a brief summary is required so that we may be able to
learn from the extant literature on South Asian rural women.

Women are not a homogeneous group

One of the first things that is clear is that one must be very
careful about treating women as a homogeneous category. Rural
women are not a single group. This may seem a truism, but the
number of times that writers on women do not make clear regional,
class, religious or age distinctions when discussing women is
surprising.

To begin with, in South Asia there are strong regional differences to be found in the way that women participate in economic
activities outside the home, and in decision-making within the
household and on farm management issues. A few examples should
suffice. Albrecht in a review of the living conditions of rural
families in Pakistan maintains that in Peshawar District it is
"unheard of for women of childbearing age to do field work"
(1974: 20). S. Ahmed talking about Pakistan in general claims
that women's work in sowing and harvesting is as important as
that of men's (1967: 52). Gulati points out that there is a
definite trend towards higher female participation in work outside the home as one goes from north to south and from east to
west on the Indian sub-continent (1975b). Attempts to correlate
this difference in work participation rates with cropping patterns of cereals or rice on an aggregate level of interstate

comparison was not successful (Gulati, 1975a) though the analyst admitted that the State level was probably too gross for this type of relationship to show up satisfactorily.

In Sri Lanka a similar difference in women's extra-familial work participation is also found. Jungle cultivator women of the northern province do much of the slash and burn agriculture while their men do the paddy rice cultivation. "Chena work becomes a heavy responsibility of the wife" (Ryan, 1955: 154). Conversely in the Central Province, Obeysekere describes the local stereotype of women as "physically and mentally weak" supposed only "to engage in domestic activity, cook, draw water, bring firewood, and look after the welfare of children and husband" (1963: 326).

Many observers have commented on the greater mobility and independence of women in the south of India and Sri Lanka compared to women from the northern regions of the sub-continent. "In South India women are not so restricted and are not so cut off from their natal families" (Mandelbaum, 1970: 89). South Indian "women enjoy a high degree of freedom of movement" (Beteille, 1975: 64). In Sri Lanka women can make trips out of the village when they wish to visit relatives, attend the doctor, engage in money lending, invest in land, collect debts and supervise harvesting of land they hold elsewhere (Alexander, 1973: 42).

Women's informal power may differ regionally as well. Mandelbaum maintains that women in South India can dominate the domestic scene and often do (1970: 93); while Wiser says that an Indian woman is not "without certain powers, she can be careless about food purity and menstruation" (1963: 81). Ahmed, however in a Bangladesh village, paints a picture of a male dominated society where women are more closely controlled:

"As females they are thought to be physically weak and helpless and unable to defend their chastity or womanhood without the help of men and unable to earn and support themselves like men. There is little chance of their holding any social or political position inside or outside the village. The men also think of them as inferior because 'they do not understand things like men', or 'are not as intelligent as men'. Whether in family affairs or in social, political or economic life, their position is still inferior to that of men. She cannot go out to the shop, catch fish in a river or the tank, or work in the field as men can do. She is not free even to take decisions for herself, or for the family" (Ahmed, 1968: 200-201).

However, having attempted a set of generalisations about women
and their relatively different rates of work participation,
their mobility, and their share in decision-mkaing one is imme-
diately faced with the fact that these generalisations must be
adjusted again to account for local differences in cast and
class. The question of the interrelationship between caste and
class membership is a difficult one which is not within the
province of this paper. Suffice it here to say that roughly
speaking, high caste does not necessarily mean a correspondingly
high class membership. Some would go so far as to say that
class (and therefore, for South Asia, caste analysis) must be
analytically prior to any analysis of women's status vis-a-vis
men (Stoler, 1975). Other researchers such as Zeidenstien question whether this is necessary, since they argue that to some
extent women blur the boundaries between castes in a way which
men never do. However, it certainly is true that there is a
strong correlation between caste membership and the activity
of women outside the home. Bhatty calls non-Ashraf (essentially
lower caste) women "partners of their husbands in the whole
daily struggle for living" (1975: 29). Elgar (1957, 1960) writing for a Punjabi village makes clear the greater work participation of artisan women, who support their husbands in their
work, in comparison with *zamindar* (landlord caste) women whose
main task seems to be to supply hospitality for their husbands'
guests. Nath conducted a comparison of women in three different
castes in Rajasthan. Women in farmer/cultivator and untouchable
families work in the fields and in paid employment in factories,
while Brahmin women do little more than cook elaborate dishes
for their husbands (1977). Saeed (1966), in an intensive analysis of the work done by women of Janglee and refugee descent
groups in her village, comes to similar conclusions; as does
Stokes for women of different castes in India where women of
lower caste do more work than high caste women. High caste
women are described as spending the day grinding spices, wash-
ing dishes and quarrelling with one another (1975: 224). Lower
caste women thus have a stronger position in the household in
important decision-making (ibid: 200). Women who "represent
a subset of the poorest class of the rural economy of Bangladesh,
who can no longer depend on their fathers, husbands, sons or
their possessions or land" leave the home and do manual labour
on the Food for Work Programme being run by the Government"
(Chen, 1977b: 8). Ellickson points out that "women of Bangladesh are raised as dependants and learn to fear independence,
as well they might. The only relatively independent women is
the middle aged or elderly widow and divorced or abandoned
woman without male sons to support her. Here is a sad and

desperate independence" (1975: 82). In Bangladesh, as economic
status decreases, visibility increases (Alamgir, 1977: 2).
The case for Sri Lanka is not clear, but there is little that
leads one to think that the basic situation is very different.

Religion is also an important variable affecting the status
of women. In South Asia Hinduism and Islam are the two most
significant religions, though a certain number of Buddhists and
Christians also exists. Jacobson's thesis explores the differences in the instituion of purdah or control over women by family
and kin between Hindu and Moslem residents of a North Indian
village. She found striking difference in its operation, with
concomittant effects on the mobility, expectations and life
cycles of Hindu and Moslem women, including their relative
labour contributions to their natal and fmaily farms. In the
Hindu tradition, a woman practised purdah only in her husband's
home and never in her natal family; the restrictions on her mobility begin after her marriage and move to her husband's village. Moving into a house of strangers, a woman finds herself
constricted and hemmed in by strict avoidance patterns designed
to create distance between her and the male affines. As a result girls are eager to visit their natal homes and often abstract whatever surplus they can carry back to their own families.
Moslem girls observe purdah in both the natal and conjugal homes,
always wearing a *burga* (a voluminous outer garment which con-
ceals the face and body of the wearer) outside the home; when
strange men come to the house they retire to an inner room.
However, women do not have to avoid uncles, cousins and other
male affines. Moslem purdah is related to the unity of the
kindred *vis-à-vis* the outside non-kin world and helps to prevent
alienation of kingroup property through carefully arranged marriages, because Moslem women inherit property, unlike their
Hindu counterparts. As a result, Moslem girls are both more
personally restricted and more committed to their affinal families
(1970: 15-17) than are their Hindu counterparts.

The writers of *Toward Equality* lay great emphasis on the different attitudes, beliefs and practices affecting women held by
the major religions of India because "religion provides ideological bases for the accorded status and institutionalised roles
of women in a society" while the roles women play and the restrictions on them "are largely derived from the religious con-
ceptions of a woman's basic characteristics" — such as her assumed virtues, vices, strengths, weaknesses and capacities"
(Committee on the Status of Women in India, 1974: 38).

Practices and beliefs related to women held by some religious groups may even be exacerbated in certain social contexts. Vreede de Stuers (1968) is convinced that Indian Moslems are stricter than Moslems elsewhere in the treatment of their women because they are a minority group. Bhatty, in her examination of Moslem women in Uttar Pradesh, maintains that the position of Indian Moslem women is influenced by both Islamic injuctions and Hindu traditions, a fact that she feels has meant that the conservative and restrictive elements of the one have "tended to neutralise and dominate the liberal attitudes of the other" (1975: 26).

Finally, a woman's access to resources, participation in family decision-making, and mobility, are strongly linked to her age. Wiser, discussing how to achieve effective extension work in the area of child-care, hygiene or nutrition, points out that in extended households it is the older women who govern younger ones and that any attempt to bring about changes in these essentially 'women's matters' must begin by convincing these older females, rather than the young mothers (1963: 83). Stokes (1975) in her intensive case studies of women in a Bihar village shows that older women play a major role in the management of the entire household including issues of land, loans and marketing in conjunction with her husband and the eldest son. Elgar (1960), describing how the institution of *Vartan Bhanji* (reciprocal gift exchanges) plays an important role in creating social relations in a Punjabi village, says that the older women are the guardians of the *Vartan Bhanji*, keeping track of the exchanges and calculating the proper returns. Older women in both Hindu and Moslem cultures are not restricted in their movements to the same degree as young women of child bearing age, and have even been recorded as acting separately in court cases involving water rights or non-payment of bride price in the religiously conservative region of Baluchistan (Pastner, 1971: 199). Jacobson (1970) observed that both Moslem and Hindu women past middle age can move about the village, go to some feasts, and even bargain with pedlars; the fact that there are very few men in the village who are older than they is a justification for their freedom and lack of supervision. Sattar, writing about Bangladesh, says that "the amount of free time a woman has depends on her position within the family and on its economic status; it was only older women from wealthier homes who reported free time" (1975: 52).

Thus it can be seen that women in South Asia differ in terms of region, class, religion, caste and age. As already stressed,

it is very difficult to make generalisations about women. Palmer
has suggested to me that variations between categories of females
may be even greater than other differences because women take
on the structural characteristics of the husband in an exaggerated form. In other words, in the privileged sectors of the
community, the women do no work and live a life of leisure as
a matter of family honour, but in the poorer sectors of the
community, the poor women are even more overworked and under-
nourished than their men.

Women are a disadvantaged sector

Many of the studies quoted here present evidence which supports
the contention that women are a sector which is disadvantaged
in relation to men in the areas of health and nutrition, education, amount and productivity of work. I have chosen these
limited indicators because they are non-controversial, quantitative and well documented.

In the area of health and nutrition, there is an accumulating
body of data to support the hypothesis that women are an un-
healthy and badly nourished group compared to men. The fact
that there are more men than women in many countries in South
Asia is accounted for by higher female infant and adult mor-
tality (Committee on the Status of Women in India, 1974: 17;
Castillo, 1971: 3; Lindenbaum, 1974: 3). Female babies are
four to five times more likely to suffer from protein deficiency
(Dey, 1975: 71) than baby boys. As late as 1961 Bhatnagar reported passive female infanticide, where girls who fall ill are
allowed to die or get well as fate decrees with little care and
no medical attention. Schofield maintains that men receive an
undue share of family food, while pregnant and lactating women
and children may not get sufficient (1974: 25). In addition,
the demands on constant pregnancies obviously take an immense
toll on the women's health.

Women, generally speaking, have been excluded from the advantages
of modern education. With the exception of Sri Lanka their
literacy rate is appallingly lower than that of men. 1963
figures for Pakistan (Akhtar, 1963) reveal that in East Pakistan
(now Bangladesh) 26% of men were literate compared with 8% of
women; the respective percentages for West Pakistan men and
women were 20% and 6%. If the urban sector was excluded the
rates would be lower and the gap between the sexes greater.

The Committee on the Status of Women in India reported that in
the 1969 Census, 18% of all women were literate, but only 13%
of rural women were so. The rate of all men was 39%. Bangladesh shows a low literacy rate even when compared to other Moslem countries (Smock, 1977: 105). The only exception is Sri
Lanka where, though women's literacy rate lags behind that of
men, it is so high as to make the gap less critical. 75% of
Sri Lankan women and 89% of men are literate. Despite large
funds being spent on school buildings and official concern for
the lack of education of women, the enrolment of rural girls
continues to be lower than that of boys. In Bangladesh only
21% of rural girls were registered while 46% of boys attend
school (Jahan, 1975: 8). Girls drop out much earlier than boys.
For example, in India 66% of the 6 to 11 years old girls are
registered, wheras for the 11 to 14 year olds, the figure is
22% (Rai, 1975: 18).

The reluctance to educate girls stems from several factors.
First, since most marriages in South Asia are virilocal, the
education of a girl is a financial loss to her natal family.
As Anwar pointed out for Pakistan, it is thought that "boys'
education is an investment, girls' education is passed to the
husband" (1976: 19). Secondly, a girl's labour in the household and in child-care may be very important, especially in
families where women have to spend a portion of the day in the
fields. Anwar found this to be the case in her village (op.
cit: 28) as did Nath (1977: 11). In addition, Nath's cultivator
informants explained that not only was the girl's labour necessary to cook and care for siblings while the mother worked in
the fields, but also that education was undesirable because it
spoiled women and made them want to act like high caste women
(i.e. do no work). Women's right and proper work in the fields
and in the home was such that she could do it just as well without any education.

It must be obvious from even a brief perusal of some of the
time allocation data presented in the following section on the
importance of women's work, that women in the village work very
hard, sometimes even harder and longer than the men of the
family. This is true even in South Asia where women's work
contribution is not as dramatic as that of African rural women.
Where a woman contributes extensively to economic activities
outside the home, she still has many domestic and childcare
duties, since men rarely help in the home. Even when she only
works within the home, her days are long and full, as Schoustra-
van-Beukering's daily time allocation for a Bangladesh woman

shows (1975: 58-9) (reproduced in Appendix 1). Men's days are
shorter. When the work in the fields is over, men find time to
smoke or play cards under a tree (Chakravorty, 1975), or as
M. Dube has told me, they go visiting. Farouk in his survey of
time allocation in a number of Bangladesh rural and urban areas
concludes that "housewives have to put in between about 10 to
13.6 hours daily in all kinds of productive work; this is also
more than the work done by the male heads of families" (1976:
73). These strictures apply more to wives of farmer cultivators
and landless labourers than they do to wives of large landowners and landlords. As Nath shows in her study among women
of three castes in Rajasthan, Brahmin women spend large portions
of the day cooking. As I pointed out earlier it is difficult
to generalise about South Asian women for they are part of many
diverse economic and social patterns affecting their many roles.

Not only do women work very hard, often too hard and long, but
also the work they do is of low productivity. "Men have been
recruited to modern and urban-based occupations and their productivity in the output and marketing of surplus goods and services generally ignore those activities performed by women and
the subsistence commodities and services they produce. What
needs to be investigated is the effect of this relative lack of
productivity on family consumption patterns and capital accumu-
lation. It seems obvious that raising the productivity of any
family member in any activity leads to a rise in output of
family production. Productivity may even decline because women
have less access to technological training, credit and assistance (Tinker, 1976: 25).

Importance of women's work

Women's productive labour in the rural area has only recently
attracted significant attention from planners, administrators
or researchers. Not only has the female work contribution been
ignored (so that work tasks for a village are often listed without any breakdown as to which of them were done by women and
which by men) but "most anthropologists and economists have
consistently underrated the role of women as managers" (Firth,
1970: 31). As already stressed too often in South Asia, women
are considered by the statisticians and census takers as 'dependants' or 'economically inactive'. An FAO report (1976) points
out that most studies of public labour use inaccurate parameters
to estimate female work participation and that the concept of
economically inactive must be reconsidered when a closer look

is taken at the work these 'inactive' women actually do. Schous-tra-van-Beukering (1975) estimates that the women that she studied in the village in Bangladesh worked a 13.6 to 17.6 hour day. Sattar (1975) has described an average working day of a Comrilla district village women as beginning before dawn and continuing till late in the evening with no free time. Meena cultivator women in Rajasthan do more field work than their men and have full responsibility for housework and child care as well (Nath, 1977). Meena men realise that a wife is an ab-solute necessity to run a farm as well as a household. I know that Mukul Dube, doing research on rope makers in Uttar Pradesh, found that women did more rope making than their mates, while also performing their multitudinous domestic duties, and usually average a 17 to 18 hour work day.

Arjun Makhijani, a researcher working for the Foundation for Research in Community Health in Bombay, worked in a village in Maharashtra, a wet rice economy. Farmers' wives in this area begin their day at 5 a.m. to prepare breakfast and spend their days in the fields, even in the dry season when their work may be even more arduous than it is during the wet season. In the evening they must complete their domestic duties while men go and relax with their fellows, perhaps at the local tea shop. Sri Lankan women are a necessary part of the family labour team as has been shown in studies by such researchers as Pieris (1956, 1965), Leach (1971) and Newton Gunasinghe (personal com-munication). However, Sri Lankan women may contribute less direct labour to productive processes than do their counterparts in other regions of the subcontinent (with the possible excep-tion of jungle women in Sri Lanka; see Ryan, 1955). Chakravorty describes a woman's day in a village in the wheat growing area of Haryana, India:

> "A housewife has to perform more or less the same daily chores. She gets up between 4.30 and 5.00 a.m., grinds wheat, churns milk, cleans the cattle shed, milks the buf-falo/cow, feeds the animals, collects dung, prepares dung cakes, cleans the kitchen and utensils, serves the break-fasts, makes the dough for *chapatis*, prepares *chapatis* and *sabji* or *dal* for lunch. Either the women or gronw up chil-dren in the family take the cattle for *gora*, the common pas-ture found in the village. After that, at about 8.00 a.m. she goes to the field. She returns home at between 6.30 and 7.00 p.m., again carrying fuel or fodder loads on her head. She brings the cattle home, ties them, gives them food, cleans the house, goes to bring water, cooks the

Fig. 1 Indian Girl at the Village Well (Photo: Barbara van Ingen)

Fig. 2 Muslim Women Voters in India (Photo: Government of India, Publication Division)

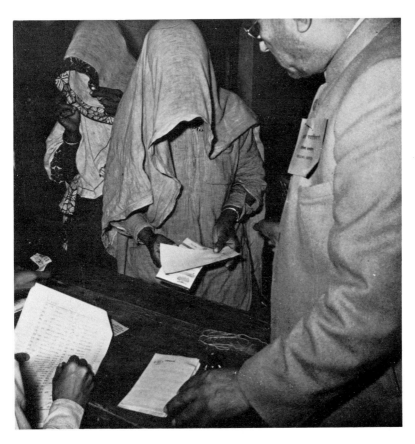

Fig. 3   Women Voting in India (Photo: Government of India,
         Publication Division)

Fig. 4   Indian Women Transplanting Rice (Photo: T. Scarlett Epstein)

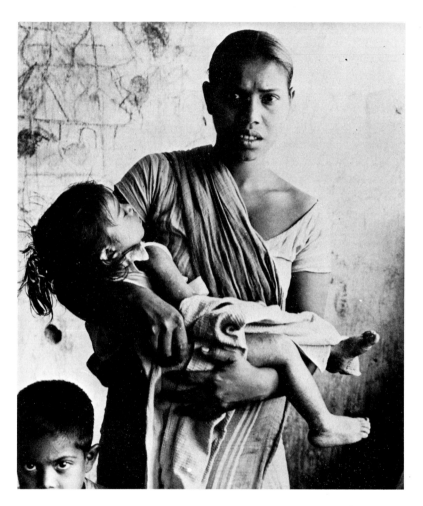

Fig. 5   Sri Lankan Mother With Her Sick Child (Photo: UNICEF)

Fig. 6   Indian Woman Operating A Village Oil Press (Photo: T. Scarlett Epstein)

Fig. 7 Indian Women Weeding Paddy (Photo: T. Scarlett Epstein)

Fig. 8 Sri Lankan Girl Cooking A Meal (Photo: UNICEF)

dinner, milks the buffalo/cow, keeps the milk on slowly over a fire for simmering, serves food to family members, takes her own meal, and sets the milk for curd. She retires to bed between 9.30 and 10.00 p.m." (1975: 9).

In a Pakistani village, where women are secluded, Khan reports that:

"A typical village woman works for 14 hours on a normal day, i.e. a day outside the hectic harvesting or sowing seasons. Of these 14 hours at least 5 hours a day are spent in animal care, collecting, carrying and preparing fodder. Other major daily activities are milking and churning, cooking and carrying food to the fields. Planting, harvesting and processing seasons intensify the physical chores of the village women. During the wheat harvest for example, women spend about 10 hours a day in the fields. They help their husbands in rice transplanting and sowing. Picking cotton and chillies are also major annual activities. Women living in mud houses have to renovate them twice a year after the end of the rainy seasons." (1976: 38).

Women's work is obviously extremely important to the maintenance of the family and the management of the farm, involving hard physical labour and long hours. Yet at the same time women's work is often not recognised either by local men or by observers and officials. In Bangladesh:

"Women's work is mainly supplementary to that of the man. The woman processes the raw food materials he brings in, she grows the vegetables that supplement the basic meal of rice. Because of the supplementary nature of the work that a woman does, she is treated as no more than an appendage to the male family group. It is mainly because of male prejudice and men's narrow conception of productive work that the importance of her work is not recognised. It is thought that only men earn family income. Women contribute to the family income. Her hard work milling rice and grinding grain saves family money" (Arens, 1977: 41).

Constraints imposed on women's productive labour by housework, child-bearing and child-care have only recently become a concern of researchers. Many observers of rural women have shown how women must fit in labour outside the home with their family and domestic duties and child care responsibilities. As Brown has pointed out in an early article on the organisation of female

labour, women will do field work only when it is compatible
with child bearing responsibilities (1970). Mukul Dube has
illustrated the constraints on women migrating to Haryana for
paid agricultural labour; they could only go for the paddy rice
work season because this was the work that took place when
school children were on holiday and could go with their mothers
(1975). Those people interested in educating or retraining
women must take these constraints into account. Schoustravan-
Beukering points out that household tasks take most of the
woman's time and "it is difficult to divert their attention to
other matters as the household tasks are always more important"
(1975: 62). Sattar makes the same point in her review of Bangladesh village women's work. "The amount of free time a woman
has depends on her position within the family and on its economic status. Older women from wealther homes reported free
time after sunset or after the evening cooking has finished.
But on the whole the women seemed to have very little free time,
may be an hour or half an hour during the morning or late after-
noon" (1975).

There is a limited amount of evidence to show that when women
participate actively in the productive process, whether it is
on the family farm producing subsistence crops or in cash-earn-
ing activities such as wage employment or cash cropping, they
are likely to take a more active part in the allocation of
resources within the family and in family management decision-
making. Jayaramon in reviewing the workers on three tea plantations in Sri Lanka observes that the wife "being often an individual wage earner has considerable influence over the husband"
especially in the allocation of money for family expenses (1975:
134). Stokes quotes a midwife in a Bihar village as saying "I
am earning money and grain for the family, so my opinion must
carry weight" (1975: 223). In the same village Harijan women
are considered to be part of a team with the husband and are
invariably consulted by their husbands on all decisions (Ibid:
219). This was contrasted with upper caste women of the same
village where the young wives are especially isolated and not
consulted. They also perform little productive labour outside
the house. Bhatty (1976) in comparing Asraf and non-Asraf women
of Moslem India does not explicitly make the connexion between
the productive contribution of non-Asraf women, who are the
partners of their husbands in the daily struggle for earning
a livelihood, and their relatively less subordinate position
compared with men. However, such a connexion is implicit in
her data. Nath concludes at the end of her comparison of

cultivator, Untouchable, and Brahmin women, that those of the
latter caste have a more subordinate position *vis-à-vis* men
than cultivator or Untouchable women because they make such a
small contribution to family production, depending as they do
entirely on the earnings of their employed husbands.

> "The Social position of women among Meenas and Chamars was
> superior to that among Brahmins. The ban on widow remar-
> riage and divorce, the payment of a dowry and women's sub-
> servient position generally associated with Hindu society
> exist only among Brahmins. The practice among Chamars and
> Meenas is different, instead they are respected and even
> feared, almost dominant in the home" (1977: 33).

Chatterjee, in describing family division of labour among sweepers in Benares (an interesting study with much data on women,
albeit in an urban context), shows the almost symmetrical division of domestic labour in the households of sweepers where
both husband and wife were employed in the city. Whichever
spouse arrived home first would begin fetching water and cooking the daily meal (1977).

Paradoxically, women who enjoy a higher status within their own
families (i.e. having a greater say in the organisation and allocation of family resources) may have a lower status in the community because of this very economic productivity and increased
management role. This may go some way to explain why Nath
found that, despite their increased status within the home,
Untouchable women choose to stop working and become housewives
when their husbands attain a certain economic level. This question will be dealt with in the next chapter, but it is worth-
while to bear in mind here that increased responsibility and
authority within the home does not automatically lead to
greater prestige within the total community.

It is often argued that in areas where the female contribution
to agriculture is high, women are more highly valued; the indicators sometimes used are bride wealth and a high incidence of
polygamy. Women in these circumstances enjoy considerable
freedom of movement and some economic independence. Leaving
aside for the moment the controversial question of whether or
not a high incidence of polygamy indicates a relatively higher
status for women (it is possible to argue quite the opposite),
further examination of the problem reveals that it is more complex than a mere one-to-one relationship between women's economic production and their status. Many other intervening variables

must be examined, a very important one being the amount of control women have over the products of their labour. This also
raises again the thorny issue of how one measures "productive"
labour. Is the important work that Bangladesh women do in processing, preserving and storing of rice for consumption productive or not? Even cooking and fetching water is necessary and
productive when viewed from an angle of what it would cost to
purchase these essential services in the market place. Perhaps
it is a question of relative contribution or the productivity
of the contribution. Cooking and cleaning is work that is usually regarded as having low productivity compared to the labour
of men in the fields.

Women live their lives through their male relatives

Physical seclusion of women has the effect of cutting them off
from the outside world, and they can make contact with it only
through the mediation of male kin. This only holds true for
those women who have male kin to care for them, as is shown in
Chen's touching description of the woman who applied for work
under the Food for Work campaign currently running in Bangladesh,
(1977). The widows interviewed by Ellickson in a Bangladesh
village were reduced to begging and were not equipped by their
past training and experience to compete with men in daily existence. Women accustomed to being cushioned from contact with
the larger world by the walls of the *bari* (compound) are singu-
larly ill-equipped to take independent action when these walls
are penetrated by death and disaster (Ellickson, 1975: 87). The
social structures of Pakistan and Bangladesh have a built-in
need for male support and protection of females (Pastner, 1974;
Smock, 1977; Zeidenstein, 1977). Women's participation in public life is vicarious (Wilbur, 1964: 129). They do not visit
nearby towns, know little about burgeoning bureaucracies, and
are kept ignorant of men's activities in the politics of the
village (Arens, 1977; Schoustra-van-Beukering, 1975). This results in what Pastner calls negative modernisation. Baluchistan women, under strict segregation, suffer increasing isolation
and a decreasing knowledge of the legal processes and rights
available to them which have been gained in the last 100 years.
Men learn to cope with the modern world while women stay isolated in the traditional sector (Pastner, 1971: 200). In India,
among Jat women of a Punjabi village, Sridharan described how
the male co-option of the new farming technology has significantly altered power and other relationships within the family.
"In the old days, a joint family council of both men and women

had decided what crops go where and when. But farming was no
longer an extension of domestic activity" (1975: 45). Women,
hampered by purdah restrictions, poor education and household
duties "cannot cope any more with the complexities of modern
agriculture" (op. cit).

*The sterotyped household and the myth of the ever-present
male head*

Much research that has been done in assessing development projects that have already been carried out in a number of countries
points to the fallacy of thinking that women necessarily benefit from development programmes directed towards men. A number
of experts in the field of women in development have been at
pains to demonstrate that though the family may be the unit of
production, male heads of families are not the sum total of the
family. Kabir in an assessment of the Bangladesh approach to
rural women has named this as one of the 'myths' (stereotypes
about rural women) which "are barriers to creative, innovative
thought on women which must be re-examined, if not exploded,
before a strategy for the better integration of rural women in
national development can be found" (1976: 3). As she cogently
states, proponents of the 'trickle down' theory of development
who suggest that the lot of women will improve with that of men,
have sometimes been proved wrong when development activities
directed solely at male agricultural production have had a negative impact on women in the rural area (ibid: 7). Under colonial rule in many Developing Countries modernising of farming
favoured men: cash crops were introduced for men, land was put
under the private ownership of men, often dispossessing women
who had rights under traditional communal land tenure systems
(though this was more true of Africa than the Indian subcontinent), modern education and wage labour was made available to
men, and co-operatives and classes in improved production have
been offered only to men (Tinker, 1976a: 25). Women's productivity has stood still or even declined since "women have no
access to money and technology" and in some circumstances (as
I have described above) have had an increased work load (ibid:
27).

Regarding the male head of the household as representing the
household assumes that within the household (as a productive
unit) the rewards of production are equally distributed. Many
observers argue that this is an assumption that must be critically examined. For example, when food is scarce, there is

evidence that men obtain an inordinate proportion of available
food (Schofield, 1974: 25). Medical care may be more difficult
for women of the family to obtain than it is for men. Jacobson
found that only women who had had significant *Mehr* payments
could obtain medical care on demand (1970: 360). If there are
conflicting claims on family surplus, either in cash or in kind,
it is likely that male claims will defeat the female ones. Wolf
pointed out that Taiwanese women had to take money surreptitiously
from the family coffers to increase their daughters' dowries
(the size of the dowry determines the status of the incoming
bride in her new family). "The mother has no compunctions about
doing this. The father is always the manager or guardian of the
family property for future generations of males. The mother
has no such loyalty to the family" (1972: 131). If cash is
short, only boys are sent to school. Male prestige goods may
be purchased before labour-saving equipment for women's domestic tasks (T. S. Epstein, personal communication). Men may
wish to use scarce family resources on drink and other leisure
activities. Women labourers on tea plantations in India complained that their husbands had a bad habit of spending too
much of their wages on drink (Jain, 1976b).

If the purpose of development is to involve people as 'participants' in a process leading towards increased productivity, more
equitable distribution of resources, and more control by indi-
viduals over their own lives, then surely rural development
objectives must clearly include opportunities for increasing
women's active participation rather than treat them patronisingly
as beneficiaries (Kabir, 1976: 7). Women must be encouraged,
and where necessary helped, to make "a more effective contribution to capital formation, particularly to improvement of human
capital" (Germain, 1975: 2).

One should point out that though male headed households may be
the norm in most rural areas, this does not mean that all households are headed by men. Labour migration, war, famines and
changing patterns of marriage and divorce can drastically alter
the form of the rural family. In Bangladesh the Food for Work
Programme belatedly realised that many women heads of households
desperately desired to be included in the programme. The response to the opening of the programme to women was surprisingly
high (Chen, 1977). The Women's Research and Training Centre
for the United Nations Economic Commission (1975) quotes an ILO
report on Employment, Incomes and Equality as estimating that
one third of rural households could have the male head living
away in town for extended periods, or could be households in

which the husband had died or had deserted the family. Pepe
Roberts, a British antrhopologist who worked for some years on
research-action programmes in Niger, discovered that the women
who were most eager to assume leadership in projected activities
were barren, divorced or widowed. These were the very women
defined as atypical by the project organisers and were not the
ones towards whom the programmes were directed. One is led
to ask why development planners reject these rural women just
because they do not fit the preconceptions about the rural family
held by those who draw up the plans in the capital, or in another country. Such stereotyped thinking reveals a limited view
of what development is and for whom it is intended, and often
ignorance about the true state of affairs in rural communities.

Women's status and fertility

There is a certain amount of evidence that a woman's willingness
(ability?) to make fertility decisions is correlated with her
status within the community. A number of thinkers on fertility
control have put forward this type of hypothesis. "The evidence
suggests that birth rates are lower when women make decisions
about their own fertility and have the means to implement these
decisions" (Rogers, 1977: 8). Making such decisions implies a
certain control over one's life. Chaudhury concludes in his
study on fertility and labour force status, that agricultural
employment has a negative effect on fertility, while housework
does not (1974). The question this conclusion raises is the
interesting one of whether or not women's economic activities
outside the home have any effect on her fertility. If a woman
has a role to play earning income for her family either in the
traditional or the modern sector this could mean that her status
in terms of decision-making power within the family may be increased. One must be careful not to read too much into Chaudhury's conclusions, since the only women in Bangladesh who work
are those from the lowest economic brackets, and one cannot
discount the possibility that poverty (with inadequate diet) may
have a depressing effect on fertility. Mukerjee, presenting
some data on women's fertility in India (Haryana, Tamil Nadu
and Meghalaya) emphasises that women's status may be an important variable. Her summary of research on village women and
their fertility in Kenya, Mexico and the Phillipines demonstrates
that fertility behaviour is very complex and differs in different places for different reasons. Nearly everywhere motherhood
is valued and the number of children may not necessarily be a
determinant of status but *vice versa* (1977). Dixon (1977)

advocates income generating activities for women in rural areas
based on the assumption that these give women both increased
status within the home and a more positive self image such that
they may feel better able to make important life decisions
(i.e. determining family size).

Another variable sometimes connected with family planning acceptance is women's education. M. Das Gupta argued that the educational level of women was strongly correlated with fertility
behaviour and beliefs in a village in Delhi State. Education
raises the age of marriage, and increases the chance that women
will gain employment outside the home, and, as she sees it,
employed women will have less time to spend raising children
(1975). Again one must be cautious in assuming too much without further data. The correlation between education and fertility may relate more to the raising of the age of marriage
than to any particular increase in women's status due to education.

*Some of the effects of "development" on the roles of
rural women*

In this section I briefly cite the already recorded effects of
past rural development on the roles that women have played in
the socio-economic life of the village. Some of these results
appear contradictory: changes have brought about different
results in different contexts. New technology has often replaced women's productive roles. This can be because time-sav-
ing mechanised means have been introduced to do the work which
women used to perform more laboriously. In almost no case do
women have access to the operation and control of these technological innovations. For example the introduction of plough
cultivation meant replacing women's work (hoeing) and the co-
option of the new technology by men (Goody, 1973; Boserup, 1970),
though there is no real reason why women should not be able
to handle the plough. More recently, herbicides have deprived
women of incomes from weeding in large parts of South Asia
(A.D.C., 1974). Rice mills and large scale parboiling and dry-
ing equipment in Bangladesh have begun to replace traditional
women's work. Many poor women have lost a source of income.
This "raises the spectre of the devaluation of women at a time
when there is some evidence that their economic status is already in decline" (Lindenbaum, 1974: 3). The same phenomenon
has been described by Barbara Hariss for South India (1977).
Capital-intensive rice milling installations hire very few

workers (mostly men) and replace productive work once done by
women. The Green Revolution, so successful in such areas as the
Punjab, has been accompanied by a rapid withdrawal of women from
the 'active' work force (Asian Regional Workshop, 1976; Billing,
1970; and Nath, 1970).

> "The elimination of farmwork in the Punjab (picking fodder,
> picking cotton or vegetables, collecting fodder for animals)
> and lighter domestic work (due to mechanised grinding of
> corn, domestic hand pumps) have given women a lot of time,
> which they are devoting to cooking, better care of the home,
> themselves and their children, practising traditional crafts
> such as durry making and learning new ones such as knitting
> and sewing" (Nath, 1965: 814).

While in one sense one can only be glad that some of the
work load has been removed from women, often already overworked,
in another sense this trend is disturbing. The response of many
women in rural villages of South Asia to income-earning programmes indicates that rural women may want cash and/or other
income more than free time (Dixon, 1977). Admittedly this is a
question which requires examination. Observers of the development scene are increasingly concerned that where technology
frees women from time consuming, arduous or unproductive tasks
there are no viable alternative forms of productive work for
them. The Reading Paper No. 458 of the International Women's
Year Seminar (1975) expresses this concern. While women are
being released from such tasks as water carrying, rice husking,
wheat grinding, spinning, and feeding cattle, there were no
serious productive alternatives being offered. Thus development may drive women out of economic production entirely. This
can only have adverse effects on a nation's socio-economic
health (Zeidenstine, 1975).

Development can also deprive a woman of her previously productive roles in a less direct way: namely when manufactured goods,
either imported from abroad or manufactured by investors in the
metropolis, replace the craft goods that women were making in
the home for use or exchange. Cloth, straw mats, pottery, sugar
(jaggary) are among the items that have been displaced by manufactured equivalents in South Asia. Not only do women lose an
important productive role within the family unit as well as a
possible source of cash or exchange value, but also the family
must now part with cash to acquire the higher prestige and more
expensive replacements (Bossen, 1975; Germain, 1975; Nash, 1977).

Technology can, in certain circumstances, have a different but
equally disturbing effect on women's work roles in rural areas.
Rather than mechanising and easing women's work it can often increase their work load. Very little specific research has been
done on this topic in South Asia; but there is data to be found.
For example, on tea plantations of both India and Sri Lanka
women employees do much more work than their husbands (Jain,
1976b; Jayaramon, 1975).

A work day for women plantation workers from 4 a.m. to midnight
is not uncommon. In Bangladesh the introduction of new High
Yielding Variety rice strains, without any concommitant explora-
tion into the effects of higher yields on the traditional home
based women's processing of rice, resulted in great floods of
rice descending on the unprepared wives of larger landowners.
Martius Von Harder has tried to show some of the effects this
increased production could have on village women (1975). In
one Bangladesh village, a researcher observed that polygamy was
on the increase among larger prosperous rice farmers for the
simple reason that they needed more than one wife to cope with
increased rice yields (Shireen Huq, personal communication,
see also p. 17).

Despite the importance of women's labour in most rural economies,
they are largely ignored by those agencies and extension workers
interested in changing patterns of production in rural areas.
Again there is no particular study of women and agricultural
extension workers done in South Asia as there has been in Africa
(Smithells, 1972). However, there is no reason to believe that
the situation is any different on the Indian sub-continent.
Observations by certain writers confirm this. Sridharan, in an
article in *Indian Farming* (1975) was puzzled why women were not
interested in the new farming techniques. He found in his ex-
plorations of the problem in a Green Revolution village that
agricultural extension work was a male process with visits from
male experts who only contacted husbands and distributed pamph-
lets which women could not read anyway. The pattern he described
does not differ from the pattern which both Smithells and Dey
find common to most rural extension programmes. Extension workers
contact only male heads of households (Smithells, 1972). This
means that widows or wives of migrants have less chance to learn
about new farming methods than residents' wives; but even they
learn little when the men do not divulge know how of the new
techniques (Dey, 1975: 47-48). Alamgir makes the same point
for Bangladesh, and gives an example of how this male orienta-
tion can have immediate and concrete effects on a programme

designed to increase production. In one such programme, the
extension workers met with and trained the male heads of households in how to preserve and store the new High Yielding Grain
for plantation purposes. This task, which was traditionally
done by women, was not completed by the men, neither did the
heads of households bother to pass the new methods on to their
wives. As a result there was not enough seed grain in the following year (1977: 67). Ignoring women in the farming process
can only lead to the increasing inefficiency of the family production unit, and a widening productivity gap between men and
women.

Epstein also gives a brief example of how ignoring women's
work roles can act as a constraint on increasing production.
Fieldmen of the Mysore Agricultural Department had convinced
farmers that Japanese-style paddy rice planting meant higher
yields. Yet not a single man had used the method despite the
incentive of credit facilities offered to enterprising farmers.
The difficulty proved to be that the contracted-out teams of
women paid labourers were accustomed to a traditional method
of transplanting where they were paid by the job. Naturally
they were reluctant to learn a difficult, tedious, more time
consuming method without an increase in pay (1962: 64).

Where development officials and experts have considered women,
it has more likely than not been in some sort of special women's
programme. Such programmes are funded on pin money compared to
the programmes directed towards men. They have the lowest budgets of any development programmes, and are often the first to
be cut when there is a financial squeeze (Dey, 1975: 48). Obviously women's programmes are not the only ones to be dissolved
or cut; it would be naive to suggest it. However, it does seem
that they are treated more casually. Some brief examples will
suffice. Gwatkin describes women's clubs which had been created
to teach proper nutrition and which had become dormant (1974:
33). Mandan describes a Women's Work Centre that had been opened
in 1955. It had taught sewing, tailoring and knitting to upper
caste women (there were organisational difficulties due to caste
prejudices). With the withdrawal of the intensive rural development programme, the extension worker departed, leaving behind
a sewing machine, a gift of the Community Development Project,
to which only a handful of women had access and knew how to
operate (1962: 9). In an Orissa village two co-operatives were
opened in 1955 making soap and tiles but these were closed due

to an inability to compete with products on the market (Patnaik, 1966: 17). In an effort to improve milk production the hiring of a 'lady social worker' in a Gujarat village brought about a 'temporary renaissance' among the village women, encouraging improved methods of cattle care and dairy procedures. Attempts were made to form a savings co-operative for women and the co-operative sale of milk, but the effort ran out of steam and the renaissance came to an end. Nanavati concludes by saying that they had to wind up the co-operative society and imputes the failure to the non co-operation of the village leaders (1961: 8-11). One is tempted to ask whether more effort, time and money could have been spent in encouraging the women to sustain their initially successful efforts to improve milk production. In *Indian Farming* Chakravorty describes a programme of agricultural extension workers to train farm women which "has not been given proper priority and has been held up for lack of funds" (1975: 53-54). Luschinsky analyses a spinning project that had been tried and failed in a Uttar Pradesh village.

> "The basic weakness of the spinning project was the inefficiency of the administration organisations. The Instructor did not appear often enough to encourage the learners. The other administrative weakness was one that is very common, the absence of adequate finance. The instructor rarely paid for the thread he received at the time he received it. The villagers lost faith in the instructor and the project" (1972: 549).

Programmes designed for women more frequently concentrate on child care and nutrition education. Even when the offer income earning activities they focus all too often on handicraft, sewing and knitting activities. The preponderance of the women's programmes in Bangladesh described by Lindenbaum (1974) fell into this category. How these products are to be marketed is not clearly thought through before the venture is begun. Many of the products encouraged either have limited market value (middle-class urbanities, or tourist) or cannot compete with cheaper factory production, because they are produced at high cost with inadequate quality control/UNICEF, 1977; Zeidenstein, 1973). In addition, women's ability to market their own products may be limited by social custom. Again in Bangladesh, purdah prevents women from entering the market place, and women must depend on their husbands and sons to market their goods. If the Integrated Rural Development Women's Programme aims to make women "economically productive and ultimately self-reliant" the ability of women to control marketing of their goods is essential (Lindenbaum, 1974: 28). Recent attempts to form women's co-operatives under the Bangladesh IRDP seem to be going some way toward accomplishing this end (Abdullah and Zeidenstine, 1978).

There are disturbing signs that when women's programmes have been successful the hostility of village men has meant that they have opposed the continuation of the programme or even in some cases, co-opted the activity for themselves. Lindenbaum described one such incident in Comilla in Bangladesh. A women's co-operative obtained a license to import coconut oil from Sri Lanka. Male relatives began to complain about the undesirable independence of women and their new 'immoral life style'. Fearing that male oppostion would jeopardise all the Integrated Rural Development Programmes, the authorities disbanded the co-operatives (1974: 29-30). Swartzberg, 1970 (quoted in Dey, 1975: 56), describes how in a Bihar village when men lost sources of cash income from selling poppies they took over the women's task of selling milk under the guise of improving their caste image. McKintosh makes the point that when men stand to gain or lose from women's participation in economic life oustide the home will largely affect their attitudes towards its reception (undated). Male opposition to new patterns of women's work participation can have disastrous results on the success of women's programmes. Failing to take this into account has undoubtedly contributed to the lukewarm reception of many programmes introduced so hopefully.

I have here examined briefly what has been learned so far about rural women and the ways in which 'development' has affected them. It must be added that most of it leads to tentative hypotheses which have not yet in any way been 'proved'. Further work needs to be done in all these areas in order to clarify the correct relationship between relevant variables and to refine those hypotheses which have been applied too generally.

Chapter IV

If More Knowledge Is The Answer, Then What Are The Questions?

More questions have been raised than we have adequate information to answer. It is agreed by most observers of the international development scene that more knowledge is essential, and nowhere is this more the case than in the area of rural women and their involvement with rural development programmes. If more knowledge is the answer, then it is vital to consider what questions could be asked by researchers anxious to make a contribution to the field of women and development.

I am aware that I am not the first to pose prospective areas for future fruitful research. There are a number of excellent papers which have done so already. For Bangladesh, Germain (1976), Zeidenstein (1977) and Alamgir (1977) have between them compiled a daunting list of possible topics that need to be explored further, with special reference to women and rural development. Papnek has produced an interesting article on issues and research on women in South and South East Asia, though her focus is more general than that of rural women or women in development (1975). Achola Pala has summed up research trends and priorities past and future for African women in rural development (1976). There are also publications that raise questions about future research priorities for Third World women generally, for example, the Agricultural Development Council's conference on "Prospect for Growth with or without the Active Participation of Women" held in 1974, or Ester Boserup's UN pamphlet on the *Integration of Women in Development* (1975), or the Special Issue of *Les Carnets de l'Enfance* "Planning with Rural Women" (Epstein, 1977).

In what follows I compile a selective list of the topics I consider to be the most urgent areas of possible research. It cannot be exhaustive; these are merely a number of possible areas where development problems need examination and where fruitful theoretical hypotheses could be tested.

Both action-orientated research (including evaluation of on-

54

going or past development projects) and theoretical research
must be done. Not only that but there must be some feedback
between the two types of research. It is desirable to make
theoretical and fundamental research relevant to the information
needs of those who must plan and implement programmes. There
must be more appropriate studies where the questions relevent
to development projects or planners can be explored and explained
without great expense and much time. Much of the research that
has been done in the past may have resulted from theoretical
concerns and been based on procedures of research that have
served the ends of foreign Universities rather than the needs
of the host country (Sondra Zeidenstein, personal communication).

Action-orientated research

Female labour participation: One of the most important areas
for consideration is that of women's participation in the rural
economy: their participation in various aspects of the agricultural process, the domestic work they do, the processing
and storing of food, and the production of goods and services
either for use or for exchange. Though, as I stated above,
there exists some data on this area, much of it is impressionistic and very sporadic. B. Dasgupta complains of the shortage
of village studies concentrating on or even devoting much attention to quantitative aspects of female labour input and time use
(1977: 278). Many intensive village level studies need to be
carried out over a full agricultural year in a number of villages
in different regions, with different ecologies and cropping patterns, as well as different cultural traditions. It is important to understand the economic role that rural women perform;
the way in which their role is, or is not, complementary to
that of their husbands, and the extent to which female labour
determines the family's productivity.

It is also necessary to understand the sexual division of labour
within the family as productive unit and the nature of the social
relations which it reflects. In addition, the control of resources (land, cash, labour) within the family must be fully
comprehended. In the various productive work tasks it will be
important to note who initiates and who controls the labour
process and the means by which the product is distributed
(Kate Young, personal communication).

Moreover, it is essential to have detailed information on the
relative access women have to information channels, extension

services, training, credit and marketing facilities. If women
do particular tasks in the rural economy, why should they not
have direct and adequate support from government agencies, just
as men get? As Kabir stresses, "rural women in Bangladesh are
major contributors to agricultural and household production
receives less recognition than their domestic and child-rearing
chores" (1976: 4). She concludes that "one pre-condition for
designing effective development programmes is to give due
attention to the actual and potential role of women in economically productive work" (op. cit).

It needs to be stressed that this data must be detailed and not
consist simply of impressionistic statements such as are obtained
in surveys in answer to questions about "women's work" and
"men's work". One way that this research could be carried out
is by collecting time allocation information for all members of
sample households. It is important to know not only what household members actually do but also the relative time allocated
to particular tasks. Furthermore, these types of studies should
be sequential observations of the same households over long
periods of time at different seasons of the year. It is only
in this way that it would be possible to pinpoint the constraints
of family labour, male and female, and the competing uses of
time especially in peak work periods (Tray, 1977).

However, there are other dimensions to the constraints on
family labour, especially on women's labour. Thus, research
should also include a consideration of the effect of a woman's
age on her economic contribution within and without the home.
It has been pointed out by a number of observers of women in
South Asia, that women's roles may differ drastically with their
age. Women's mobility, participation in decision-making, control over family labour, and internal or external work contribution varies with their age and the developmental cycle of the
family. In addition, it is important to understand not only
women's own perceptions of why they allocate their time the way
they do, but also to see it in the context of the way in which
the local economy is incorporated into the larger market economy.
The bare statistics of time allocation do not convey enough
about the socio-cultural aspects of a particular pattern of
division of labour.

Greater understanding of the constraints on family labour, particularly those on women's labour which are the least studied
and least understood, will have a number of results. It will
permit planners to speculate on the degree to which "removal of

such constraints might expand the family's production of subsistence goods and services and marketable surpluses" (Weisblat,
1975: 2). In turn this should lead to appropriate technological
research which may enable village women to reduce those time constraints on their productivity which permit of a technological
solution. Examples of this type of appropriate technology are
ways to obtain clean water and fuel with a smaller expenditure
of time and energy, and easier methods of processing grain that
do not displace women from this important productive task. Cooking stoves that save fuel but are in keeping with the local
cooking methods, cheap and acceptable ways of storing grain and
new methods to process foods such as vegetables and milk are
others. Two publications recently released by UNICEF in Bangladesh (O'Kelly, 1977 and Islam, 1977) show the type of simple
practical reports which could be prepared.

In addition the greater understanding of the constraints on
women's labour will allow planners, administrators and extension
workers to devise ways and means to cope with, appropriately
alter, or work within the socio-cultural constraints on women.
When women are interested in and motivated towards certain ac-
tions, they will find ways to get around the restrictions on
their movement. If cottage industries or cooperatives have to
be sexually segregated to attract women, then planners will
have to find a way to accomplish this.

Such research would also enable planners to decide whether or
not to promote fuller utilization of labour in agriculture.
One hopes that it will result in programmes to increase female
labour participation without merely substituting female workers
for more highly paid males.

Female labour and family life: A second area of research,
closely related to the first, must be singled out for separate
consideration. It is important to see whether the fact of
women working outside the home has any significant impact on
child care, family nutrition, and other aspects of family life.
There is scanty, but inconclusive, evidence that women's work-
load in peak periods has a number of negative effects on the
domestic care of the family. Women may choose to prepare quick,
easy and less nutritious food. They may be unable to prepare
special foods for infants. The gathering of green vegetables
may be omitted; housecleaning suffers and fuel and water collection is limited (Schofield, 1974: 28). "Several village studies
show that food and cooking are closely linked with agricultural

production and that indeed neglect of cooking duties during
peak season adversely affects agricultural production" (B. Dasgupta, 1977: 26). In cultural settings where men are unwilling
to assist in cooking and food preparation, the full brunt of
such work falls on women and girls.

But is it possible that women's work participation outside the
home can have repercussions other than nutritional ones? There
is evidence (again sporadic and inconclusive) that the demands
on women's work participation outside the home can have negative
effects on girls' ability to go to school. As Nath so lucidly
showed in her comparison of three caste groups, those women who
had to do a lot of work out side their homes were the ones who
did not send their daughters to school. It was the Brahmin
caste that sent their daughters to school, and in this caste
women did not work outside the home (1977). In a Bangladesh
village described by Arens "small peasant girls are needed less
for work than boys (and) twice as many girls as boys go to
primary school. Girls are sent to school if there is not too
much work to be done at home" (1977: 42). In Bangladesh, women
do not often work outside the home, and there may be less need
for girls to perform domestic tasks. Encouraging women to
greater work participation outside the home may be accomplished
at the expense of another development goal, that of increased
education for girls, unless new institutional arrangements are
made for the care of small children and easier ways of accomplishing household tasks are devised.

Finally it is necessary to pursue the whole issue of women's
formal work outside the home and its relationship to fertility.
Dixon is convinced that work participation is correlated with
lower fertility and uses this hypotheses as a justification for
a policy stressing programmes designed to increase women's productivity outside the home (1977: I-2b). However, one must be-
ware of making facile correlations. As N. Shah has pointed out
"employed women in general have higher education than unemployed
women" (1977: 20).

Women's role in household management: More needs to be known
about women's roles in farm management, money management and
other family decision-making processes (marriage, divorce,
fertility etc.). The literature available on this aspect of
rural social life is almost non-existent. Such data as does
exist is frequently vague and impressionistic, though admittedly
researching this area presents many difficult methodological

problems. Arens describes how Jhagrapur women's "horizons are
restricted mainly to their own little world and that they do
not even know approximately how much land husbands own and where
their fields are" (1977: 60). Martius-von-Harder found that
women could not answer questions on land, rental land, cropping
patterns, acreage and agricultural methods (1975). Women in a
central Indian village were found to have an ambiguous position
in family decision-making. In 74% of the households, women actually keep household money in their hands, though it is not for
their personal use. The possibility for independent purchases
depends on age, position in the family and the confidence of
the individual woman (Jacobson, 1970: 289). Women never buy
land or cattle on their own, only through male relatives. When
a man buys land or cattle, he may consult his wife, but many do
not (op. cit: 290). Hashimi, talking about women in West Pakistan, says that they play a significant role in decision-making
and that their attitudes and values greatly influence the adoption of improved implements, seeds and fertilisers (1968: 16).
This is a generalised statement and no primary data is offered
to prove this assertion. By way of contrast Pastner recounts
that Baluchistan women from West Pakistan lead restricted lives,
contribute little to the economy, are isolated in the household,
and are passive participants in alliances between domestic groups
(1971: 148).

Even allowing for regional, cultural, wealth, and age variations
in women's roles and status, these contradictory statements need
to be reconciled or explained by further research. Women may
have no recognised public role in decision-making, but they may
exercise more informal control over decision-making than has
been recognised in the past. Those researchers who have done
intensive examinations of village women have sometimes revealed
the informal, domestic mechanisms utilised by women in the domestic group. Pastner describes the covert methods women use to
accommodate purdah: they deny their husbands sexual favours,
they coax, quarrel and complain, refuse to cook and fake illness.
They form alliances among themselves and gain their ends by surreptitiously manipulating male members of the household (1974:
412). Jacobson devotes a large part of a chapter to women's
decision-making power. It varies with a women'as personal
wealth, her family's status, her age, her position in the family
development cycle, her health, her confidence, her knowledge
of the world and agriculture, her mobility (Hindu women know
more village gossip than Moslem women since they move around
their village more) and her work. Rich families have bigger
decisions to make and a woman with substantial *mehr* payments

can get medical aid without permission. Old women's advice is
more sought after. Wives in nuclear families have more influence than women of similar age living in extended families.
Clever women can influence decisions or steal grain or money
from the family coffers (1970: 300-369).

Knowing more about the roles women play in family management,
their own perceptions of them, and the methods they utilise to
accomplish their ends should enable planners and others interested in involving all people in the development process to capi-
talise on women's decision-making powers and capabilities. It
should also lead to new methods of mobilising women, especially
when the socio-economic variables which favour strong decision-
making roles by women are clarified.

Women and consumption patterns: There are some hints in the
available literature that women have a different attitude to
the allocation of economic resources at their command than do
men. Some writers think that in contrast to men, women are more
likely to translate their economic resources (especially cash)
into basic needs for the family than into consumer and prestige
goods. Alamgir says that women perceive men as squandering
money even where savings are small. Forence McCarthy makes the
same observation (1977). She found that women participating
in the relief programmes use their money for household affairs
and necessities, education, health, clothing for children, small
livestock, and small business ventures. It would be interesting
to have some comparative data on how Bangladesh men spent similar incomes. It is Zeidenstein's opinion that women will be
more likely to use money for family needs (personal communication). Palmer thinks that the United Nations Basic Needs Approach is nothing more than a recognition of the fact that women
have greater concern for the needs of their family (1977). This
is especially true where men migrate to the cities to work and
tend to use more and more of their earnings to maintain and en-
tertain themselves in the urban area (Palmer, personal communication). Certainly in my own research in Kenya I found that
men who migrated to town alone, leaving their wives and families
in the rural area, spent most of their salaries on clothes,
daily subsistence, drinking and town women. Their contributions
to the rural home did not automatically go up as salaries or
earnings increased. Where subsistence economies are incorporated into cash economies, and subsistence agriculture is replaced
or complemented by cash cropping or other cash earning activities, it often happens that there is a shift in consumption

patterns: men obtain the cash and spend it on consumer goods.
Nash describes such a transition in Mexico where a sawmill provided employment for the family men. "Whereas women customarily
received the cash for crops and took care of family needs with
it, men were reluctant to relinquish their wages. It resulted
in greater drinking, and increased purchases of radios" (1977:
173). Jain was told by women labourers on Indian tea plantations that they spent their money on food while the men spent
theirs on drink (1976b: 49). Further studies are needed to as-
certain whether there is a difference in the spending and saving
patterns of men and women, and the variables with which these
differences may be correlated.

Women and the new technology: A lot of new technology and many
new institutions have been introduced into rural economies in
the last hundred years. Most of these have not been directly
concerned with women or women's work. However, since women are
part of the rural economy and the rural social structure, it is
obvious that these technological changes have had at least an
indirect effect on women. It was not until recently that techni-
cians, sociologists, economists, and development planners realised that changes in technology can often have considerable
repercussions on women's work, women's participation in the rural
economy and women's position in the family and the community.
At the same time, development experts have rarely bothered to
focus on ways of easing women's work. Further research is needed
to identify the priorities and the spin-offs of various technological innovations that would relieve women of the heaviest
tasks (like water carrying). This would enable women to work
fewer hours, and liberate them from some of their worst drudgery, while at the same time raising their food output through
greater efficiency rather than increased work. At the same time
it could provide more income earning opportunities (ILO, 1975).

There has been some village level research on the unintended
effects of technology on rural women, much of which I have already mentioned. To illustrate this point further, I give a
few more examples: rice milling machines replace women in
traditional rice milling methods (Hariss, 1977; Martius-von-
Harder, 1975; Zeidenstine, 1975). The introduction of chicken
farming in Zaire was directed solely towards the men in a Zaire
village. The planners had not considered the fact that water
was scarce in this area, that women had to carry it from long
distances and that chickens need a great deal of water. Therefore, women had several hours a day of additional water-carrying
work added to their already crowded schedules.

Thus new technologies can either deprive women of important productive roles or can increase their work load unreasonably. If planners are unaware of the possible repercussions of such technological changes, nothing can be done to provide women with alternative forms of productive work, or to try and off-set sudden increases in work-load in already busy schedules.

In addition assessments must be made of past and present development programmes with regard to their expected and unexpected effects on the women in the area covered. Very few development programmes actually consider women's needs and there are often unexpected results. These need to be examined and explained so that, in the future, planners will ensure that proper attention is given to the female half of a target population, no matter how 'unfeminine' the subject matter of the programme.

Specific women's programmes: A related topic of study must be the assessment of programmes that have been especially set up for women. Very little of such assessment is available, though a number of such studies have been done in Bangladesh, but many of them are disappointingly uncritical. All of these have already been mentioned: Abdullah and Zeidenstine, 1978; Alamgir, 1977; Chen, 1977; Germain, 1976; Kabir, 1976; Lindenbaum, 1974; UNICEF, 1977; Zeidenstein, 1975, 1976 and 1977. I could find no such evaluation of women's programmes for any other South Asian country except for Olin's paper (1976b) on the family planning programme in India and Dixon's report (1977) which includes Indian as well as Bangladesh, Pakistani and Nepalese programmes. Does this reflect the lack of concern of funding agencies and planning administrators, or the blindness of academics and academic organisations to this fruitful area of applied research? Is applied research regarded as lacking in academic prestige?

Many observers of the development scene have commented on the fact that too many programmes specially devised for women have, in Ester Boserup's words, "suffered from the weakness of being focused exclusively on women's domestic responsibilities. Meanwhile nothing has been done to improve their earning power or to integrate them in the efforts to modernize the rural economy. There is a continuing need to pay special attention to women's roles as mothers and homemakers, though care must be taken not to make this area society's exclusive concern for women" (1975: 36). Special programmes must be assessed in greater detail to drive home the point that more research, more funds and more

attention have to be directed towards the good of increasing
women's productive roles and relieving domestic drudgery. "The
increased participation of women in development is closely tied
to the provision of certain basic physical amenities, i.e. water,
fuel and sanitary facilities, and a network of public services
at the grass roots level" (Olin, forthcoming, p. 8). Basic
Needs approaches represent an attempt to make a genuine social
redistribution of resources. Because these approaches entail
providing basic services that are mainly used by women in their
roles as family maintainers, they are quite rightly seen as programmes with a direct effect on the women and children of a population. These Basic Needs programmes need to be examined, as
do the long term results on women's lives in the target area.

Programmes that have been directed towards women and their income earning potential have often been poorly thought through
and badly managed. They have frequently involved craft production for non-existent or fickle foreign or tourist markets, or
production without much consideration as to quality control,
storage or distribution of the finished goods. If women's productive potential is going to be significantly increased, then
substantial market research by experts rather than well meaning
amateurs must be conducted to ensure that the project makes use
of local materials, and will be compatible with local ideas and
could either supply local markets or could increase the consumption of the family (as in market gardening projects or egg or
milk production schemes). There is a need to co-ordinate different organisations and agencies both to share information and
to avoid wasted effort. More detailed critical studies on the
lines of the ones cited above for Bangladesh could pin-point
such wasted effort (Abdullah and Zeidenstein, 1978; UNICEF,
1977). Dixon's long report gives an excellent discussion of
the necessary economic considerations when setting up successful small rural industries for women (1977). UNICEF (Dacca,
1977) has carried out a critical assessment of similar small
industries for women in Bangladesh. Their criticisms are similar to those stated above.

It does little good to increase women's productive potential
without at the same time enabling them to control at least the
additional output (Lindenbaum, 1974: 31). In South Asia it is
often difficult, if not impossible, for women to market their
own goods. Ways and means must be explored, and reported upon,
to mobilise women in co-operatives which will give them the
social backing necessary to counter male opposition to new patterns of behaviour and production and to gain through group

action the control over their resources that individual women
could not hope to achieve alone. It is noteworthy that many of
the women's programmes in Bangladesh encourage the individual
members of the co-operatives to save through them (Abdullah and
Zeidenstien, 1978; Kabir, 1976). This undoubtedly prevents the
women's family from consuming her income as she earns it. Not
only does this enable the woman to retain the money for her own
use, but it also encourages her to save it until it can pay for
a substantial capital investment, such as some livestock, rather
than frittering it away in small purchases of food. Research
into women's savings co-operatives should be studied closely so
that there could be feedback on how well they work and how they
could be improved. Do they accomplish their task of increasing
women's productivity and their control over it? Abdullah and
Zeidenstein conclude that since all of the loans taken in the
first two years of Bangladesh's IRDP women's co-operatives have
been paid back and more applied for, productivity must have increased (1978: 235).

Extension services to women also need improving. Where cultural
inhibitions restrict contact between strange men and women, then
women extension workers must be used. Unfortunately these same
countries have restricted women's mobility, thereby making it
difficult for women extension workers to be accepted. In Bangladesh it has been discovered that women extension workers can
travel and live together in distant villages in pairs, thus
eliminating local hostility and suspicion (Kabir, 1976: 14,
Appendix). The IDRP women's programme there has arranged for
educated female staff to go to villages and help the women organ-
ise themselves into co-operatives. Abdullah and Zeidenstein
(1978) give us one of the few available reports on such a training programme, its difficulties, successes and failures. The
training of local midwives or older respected women in a village
as organisers of co-operatives or mothers' clubs has also been
reported in Bangladesh (Rahman, 1975). Wiser recommended the
use of older women in extension programmes in India (1963). In
Pakistan the midwife training programme was a start in capital-
ising on the skills of older women (Gardezi, 1969). So that the
present position can be properly assessed, in-depth studies
should be made of some of these projects and their different
approaches to the mobilisation, reaching and training of village
women.

The list of possible areas of action-orientated research is end-
less. The items mentioned here seem to be of high priority;
they are quite specific in nature. The next section puts

forward suggestions for research of a more general theoretical
nature which I suggest can also be of great importance to the
pragmatically orientated planner or administrator who wishes
to have a thorough understanding of some of the socio-economic
and ideological constraints which may prevent women from total
involvement in development programmes.

Theoretical research

Socio-historical studies: Detailed socio-historical comparisons
can play a role in the examination of regions, the transition
from subsistence to market economies, the introduction of cash
crops, and modern agricultural methods and their effect on women's
position in the domestic productive unit and the economy as a
whole. Certain theorists interested in historical analysis of
women's position have maintained that the transition from subsistence to market economy, often associated with the spread of
capitalism, has universally meant the worsening of women's status; something along the lines of Engles' World historical defeat
of the female sex. If one is interested in eliminating a system
of sexual imbalance, then it is necessary to know the base on
which this system rests. Following this line of reasoning,
Achola Pala in her article on priorities for research on African
women devotes approximately two thirds of it to a discussion of
what is and is not known about the role of women in the context
of pre-colonial African economies and the changes in women's
roles brought about by the introduction of the colonial cash
economy (1976). There is a need to locate and collate existing
data for particular regions. Many accounts (village studies,
early travellers' observations and official surveys or censuses)
may exist but a lot of work and perseverance is required before
they can be identified and rendered comparable. For example,
Vina Mazumdar, an economist working with the Indian Council for
Social Science Research, has recently been involved in an intensive analysis of old censuses, and claims (personal communication) that she has shown satisfactorily that Indian women used
to play a much larger role in rural craft production and marketing than they do today — something that has hither to escaped
the notice of most Indian historians. This type of study promotes greater understanding of the impact of the market system,
capitalist institutions, and new technology on women's roles
in the past. It may also, as in the case of Mzumdar's work,
permit one to explode preconceptions about what women did in the
past which are then used to establish precedents for what they
should now be doing.

The subordination of women: There is a great deal of discussion
in the literature on women (most of which does not deal specifically with Third World women or women in rural development) as
to the question of their subordination. How one approaches the
subject of women in any context depends greatly on the theoretical position one takes. Some people (e.g. Rosaldo, 1974) perceive a universal domination of women by men in all situations
and under all socio-economic conditions. Another member of this
school, Rubin, sees sexual oppression as a universal and not
historically specific phenomenon, while kinship systems are seen
to be based on the exchange of women (1975). However, there are
others who reject this vision of human society as being wholly
divided into male oppressors and female oppressed: "To assert
that all men are oppressors and all women are oppressed is to
dehumanize both sexes" (Nelson, C., 1977: 26). Other scholars
argue that the relationship between the sexes in traditional
societies (however these are defined) or in the subsistence
economies, represent complementary roles rather than the subordination of women. Jacobson's exposition on Indian women reveals this approach: men and women's economic roles support and
complement one antoher, and women have their sphere of influence
which is no less important than that of men (1974).

Other scholars make a case for women having significant, if covert, power over decision-making and distribution of family resources. Rogers maintains that women control the major portions
of important resources and decisions in most peasant societies
and that "a myth of male dominance is acted out" in most societies where relationships are face-to-face and production is do-
mestically orientated (1975: 728). Nelson regards Egyptian
women as information brokers, mediating between social relationships within the family and between families and the larger
society. Though Egyptian women are secluded, they have real
power in the form of their solidarity groups, their magical influence over men, their ability to shame men and to control
alliances of political power (1977).

The whole question is dauntingly complex, necessitating the
unravelling of the various historical, economic, and cultural
strands that go into making each individual situation, and then
abstracting the relevant factors for comparison on a regional
or world level. Much more research and analysis, both historical and contemporary, is needed before any firm conclusions can
be made. My perusal of the literature leads me to support the
view that the incorporation of small local economies into larger
national and world market systems has markedly worsened the

position of women, especially where production for profit rather
than for the welfare of the population has been the motivation
of governments or development agencies (Nash, 1977: 178). On
the other hand, one should not view rural women anywhere as
totally helpless in the face of complete and unreasonable subju-
gation by men, as Arens does for example when she describes
women in Bangladesh in the following terms: "Women are also
sexually exploited by their husbands. . . They serve mainly as
sexual objects to satisfy the needs of men. Men are not primarily interested in a woman as a person, but rather as a female
body. They (women) are handled as objects that can be sold or
purchased for a good price, just as a cow is traded on the market" (1977: 52-53). This view seems exaggerated, even patroniz-
ing and ethnocentric. Considering rural women's courageous and
determined struggle for survival in the face of often overwhelm-
ing odds, they cannot be viewed merely as pawns in a male power
game. Anyone who has been a member of a family understands the
real power that the modest weapons of domestic politics can
give a woman, even if she does not have direct control over the
family resources or immediate access to public channels of information and power.

A stated goal of equality for men and women does not mean that
men and women must play the same roles, and that all differences
must be swept away. With C. Nelson, I agree that the eradication of all social differentiation (between the sexes in this
case) is a goal that is neither reasonable nor attainable (1977:
26). Women everywhere must be given equality of opportunity
and choice, mobility and economic independence. Above all,
they must be encouraged to shape their own futures their own
way. This means that the whole question of subordination of
women must be explored by researchers from a subjective as well
as an objective point of view. The perceptions of rural women
themselves must be explored and their views and aspirations
must be taken into account by those extension workers, planners,
and educators who are working with rural women and who are attempting to help them mobilise themselves.

How women perceive their roles: This leads us into another
important area of theoretical research: women's attitudes to
themselves. Do rural women think of themselves as being down-
trodden, subordinate and exploited? Do they see themselves as
competitors for security in marriage? Do they feel that they
have control over some aspects of their lives and not others?
This is a difficult and ambiguous area of research, depending

as it does on individual perceptions and opinions and other areas of psychology that most social science researchers do not feel qualified to tackle. Many of the conclusions drawn by researchers in this area must perforce be extremely subjective and they may reflect as much of the attitudes and ideology of the researcher as they do those of the informants. Bearing these provisos in mind, social scientists need to set about refining current research tools to explore further the way women view themselves and the world around them. It would be interesting to know the extent to which women internalise the view of women put forward by the dominant social and religious ideologies. What are the structures which contribute to the creation and perpetuation of these self-perceptions? A related question concerns how women view men and their roles. Some of the sources cited below make tentative attempts to deal with some aspects of the problem. M. Dasgupta (1976) suggests that women in Indian villages perceive themselves as lacking control over their lives and families. Arens states much the same thing about Bangladesh women: "most of them internalise the ideas that they are inferior creatures who are dependent on their husbands and not able to do much themselves. This has led to resignation and sometimes even fatlaism" (1977: 66).

On the other hand, Pastner describes in some detail the behavioural accommodations of women in purdah which do not seem to indicate strong feelings of helplessness and inferiority. On the contrary, Baluchistan women seem quite consciously to manipulate the rules and defy men in an indirect way. Their behaviour in private belies the shy and retiring image they adopt in the presence of men; they actively participate and scheme within the family, feuding and co-operating with other women in the household (1974: 410-411). Have these women resignedly and fatalistically opted out of acting for personal ends? Omvedt has described rural women in India as being the most militant in peasant demonstrations and strikes, always in the forefront, fighting and breaking through the police lines. She related this tendency of women "to act both militantly and with a sense of the power of organisation" to the economic necessity which forced them to work for wages in the first place (1975: 45).

More research is necessary to help explain these seeming contradictions in the data, and to discover whether they lie in regional-cultural differences or in the researcher's ideological approach. This work is necessary for action personnel and administrators in order that plans and projects can be devised

which are compatible with local ideas and aspirations, including those of rural women. To ignore local ideologies is patron-
ising — imposing the views of a middle class urban elite, whether from the country of origin or foreign, on those of the rural
people — and can only be doomed to failure. Any programme which
promotes social change must take into account local attitudes
and prevailing perceptions, and the methods by which they are
transmitted and perpetuated.

How men perceive women: If women's perceptions of themselves
must be examined, so must the perceptions that men hold of women.
In socio-economic systems where men monopolise the overt public
power, it is obvious that any effort to change women's involvement in rural activities (whether in degree or in kind) will have
to deal with their fathers, brothers and husbands. The structures of family, kinship and purdah that enclose women are often
under the direction of the male heads of households. Antoun's
article on women in the Middle East examines the cultural pattern of modesty of women and relates it to a belief held by men
that women have larger sexual appetites and must be protected
since the body of the woman and the honour of the man are united
(1968: 680). The social isolation and avoidance of widows,
characteristic of traditional Hindu belief systems, is related
by Harper to the psychology of power and domination: "Groups
of adults such as women and particularly widows who lack power
and prestige and have minimal control over their own social environment are likely to be portrayed as dangerous" (1969). Dodd
conducted an interesting piece of research in Egypt in which he
proved that education has significant effects on male attitudes
to women and women's place in society. This research indicates
some of the influence that the attitudes and perceptions of men
can have on the opposition of women in society and the family.
It is important that male attitudes to women be as fully understood as female perceptions of their own roles.

Purdah: Purdah is an instituion that, as already mentioned, has
attracted a great deal of interest, especially from western
anthropologists. It is a great pity that three of the most comprehensive works dealing with the institution of purdah and the
position of women within it have not been published and are therefore not widely available, i.e. Jacobson (1970), Luschinsky
(1962) and Pastner (1971). Papanek's publications (1973, 1971)
in which she characterises purdah as a system of separate worlds
and symbolic shelter, contain the best theoretical statements

available on the subject. The practical implications of such a
system of sex segregation need to be explored further: What are
the effects of this seclusion on women's social 'visibility'?
How does it relate to their mobility, productive power and ultimately their control over their own produce? Ellickson suggests
that Bangladesh women fear to strive for independence because
the only models of independence known to village women are piti-
able widows and beggars (1975: 84). Does purdah originate in a
male attempt to control women's sexuality or is it merely a
visible expression of segregated sex roles? One answer to this
may lie in an analysis of the sanctions and pressures which ensure that the women comply with the social structures that restrict their movements outside the family or kin group. As
Zeidenstein has shown, the whole structure builds in a need for
male support, and the men can control the women by threatening
them with separation, divorce and polygamy. Women's strategies
for survival and security are aimed at the maintenance of that
male support; it is the social patterns such as obedience to
the husband and mother-in-law, and sacrifices to the son, that
are the parameters within which women have to operate when they
are engaged in the semi-secret process of formulating these strategies.

This leads us to an examination of the question, "Why do women
submit to systems of seclusion?" There are enough clues in the
existing literature to support the assertion that women themselves are often the most ardent supporters of the purdah system. Nath found that for Chamar women in India, most of whom
work outside the home for wages "the ambition of all" was to
return to the home. These women stop work whenever their husbands obtain a permanent (and therefore secure and better paid)
job in the factory (1977: 17). Bhatty states similarly that
when non-Ashraf women become richer, they aspire to act like
the Ashraf women and retire to the home. It is felt that the
highest praise one can give a husband is to say "he is able to
give his wife leisure instead of forcing her to work in the
field" (1975: 34). Helbock has also indicated that women value
purdah: "Continued urbanisation and increased education would
seem to indicate a continued lessening of the influence of
purdah, but as yet such innovative influences had little impact
on the overall situation" (1975: 19). Stress can result when
women are forced to work in those situations where the family's
economic position demands that women actively participate in
the formal wage sector as Vreede de Stuers found in North India
(1968: 87). As I pointed out earlier women obviously strive to
maintain male support, but they also seek to maintain the status

of the family in the eyes of the community. This status can be
directly translated into potential economic asset by ensuring
favourable marriages for their offspring. This is clearly illustrated by the fact that women of middle peasant families who
struggle to keep their heads above water refused to enlist in
the productive work programmes initiated in some Bangladesh
villages. The only explanation seems to be that since these
work programmes entailed leaving the home, and therefore breaking purdah, women felt the trade-off of more family income for
a loss of family prestige was not adequate to justify leaving
the home (Zeidenstein, personal communication).

If women value this institution of segregation, how can the
increase of women's participation in productive activities be
achieved? For certain segments of the population does the at-
tainment of this goal hinge on the dismantling of the purdah
system or can it be achieved within the confines of the system?
These are questions that have to be approached on a number of
different levels.

Women's structures: A discussion of purdah leads logically to
a discussion of women's social structures. It would be interesting to test the hypothesis that women's social structures
exist and run parallel to those of men. Sex segregated roles
have resulted in a relatively invisible women's life operating
behind closed doors. Very few researchers have so far managed
to enter this closed world. Maher is one, and she has written
a penetrating analysis of women's informal networks which help
Moroccan women and their children to meet their minimum requirements and to overcome social or economic crises. These networks
stem from the lack of economic autonomy of women, who only have
indirect access (through men) to the market economy. They accomplish their social and economic ends by forming and manipulating patron-client relationships between richer and poorer
women (1974). Margery Wolf studied women in a rural village in
Taiwan and found that "women's subculture is below the level of
consciousness". Women, to be successful, must learn the rules,
then how to manipulate them without seeming to do so, and then
teach this skill to their children. A successful woman is "a
rugged individualist who has learned to depend on herself while
appearing to lean on her father, husband and son" (1972: 40).
Cottam has described concealed banking systems conducted on a
surprisingly large scale by women of wealthy merchant families
in Rajasthan (unpublished).

Is it reasonable to conject, as Ardener does, a 'model of women' (women's views of women) that operates within the overall ideological framework of the dominant (i.e. male) structure (1975: xxi)? According to Ardener this women's model has often been ignored by androcentrist researchers, and often it may not be so clearly articulated as the dominant ideology. Can it also be hypothesised that these ideological 'models of women' find expression in, and/or arise out of, the social structures of women that are similarly embedded in the larger sociological framework of the dominant (male) structure? Is this more likely to be the case when a society has rigid sex-role segregation? These are theoretical questions which need further research, both at the micro-level, collecting new information from different field situations, and in comparative re-analysis of old data in order to ensure a greater understanding of women in rural society.

Women's role in society's larger institutions: family class and education

No outline of projected research on rural women can be complete without an intensive consideration of women and their relationships within the various social institutions which constitute society e.g. the family, marriage, class, schools and training centres, to name but a few.

There has already been more research carried out on women in the family in South Asia than on any other topic. Much of it has been descriptive and unsystematic and more concerned with marriage ceremonials and purdah rituals than with issues directly relevant to the role of rural women in development. The data is sporadic, making it difficult for any adequate comparative analysis to be done. Systematic work of a more intensive analytical kind is needed both in micro-level data collection and in macro-level thoeretical comparisons. Research could be conducted on topics such as domestic relationships within the household; for example, women and men's roles in household production, including access to productive resources, content and division of labour, nature of the inter-dependence of husband and wife, kinds of economic exchanges within and outside the household, and control of labour within households, biological and social reproduction of the population as well as the types of relationships which members of the domestic unit have with the public domain (Anne Whitehead, personal communication).

We need to know more of the effects of different family types
on the role and status of rural women. We should discover
whether, as Jacobson maintains, the nuclear family has a different effect on women as opposed to the extended family. She
relates women's participation in decision-making to the type of
family (1970: 300-304). This is a debate that can only be re-
solved by more comparative research. Similarly, the effect on
women of matrilineal and patrilineal kinship systems and uxorilocal or virilocal residence after marriage must also be further
explored. M. Das Gupta has put forward the hypothesis that
virilocal residence after marriage creates a situation where
brides brought from another village lack the network of natal
kin and friends to strengthen their bargaining position with
their affines. Village social structure hinges on male descended
clan groups in which "women are the moveable peripheral parts
of the community" (M. Das Gupta, 1976: 8). Men have special
houses where they meet, exchange news, make decisions for the
community, and manoeuvre politically. Women have no political
consciousness, no feelings of female solidarity, and have no
groups of their own. Margery Wolf describes a similar situation in Taiwan where the people practise virilocal village exo-
gamy. Older women form friendship groups which are powerful
protective forces for their members, but young women who have
just married into the village must become accepted by the older
women in order to become included in this collective solidarity
group that is able "to lose face for their men folk in order to
influence decisions that are ostensibly not theirs to make"
(1972: 40). Until young women are thus accepted, they are
largely defenceless. It is interesting to note that the People's
Republic of China, in their women's campaign, made an abortive
attempt to introduce uxorilocal marriage based on the assumption that this would improve the status of rural women (Elizabeth Croll, personal communication).

Women are also members of social classes. Much research is
needed in this area. For example, one could examine the economic and political changes of local class structures and the
position of women within them. Historical and sociological
studies could be conducted in areas of economic transition from
subsistence agriculture to incorporation into the larger market
systems. Some observers think, with June Nash (1977), that
when small subsistence groups become incorporated into monetar-
ised capitalist systems women of landless or small peasant
classes become increasingly overworked, while women in large
landowner classes are withdrawn from the labour force. These
propositions need further examination and explanation.

Do women belong to social classes in the same way that men do?
Do women reflect in exaggerated fashion the characteristics of
the classes to which they belong, or does women's behaviour
blur class distinctions? In other words, to what extent do
women reflect or cross class lines? Ingrid Palmer argues that
women largely reflect the characteristics common to their particular class (1975, see pp. 50-51). Zeidenstein, however, after
an experience attempting to encourage rural women to participate
in special income earning projects suggests that women do not
always act in ways consistent with their class membership (personal communication). Pastner also found that women's visiting
patterns "mitigated some of the severity of hierarchies" operating in the wider societies. Women visitors to upper class
houses reflect the full specturm of classes within the village
(1974: 412). The ranking of women in the community did not
reflect the same class factors as did men's rank, but was based
on age, fertility, personality and the status of the woman's
natal and conjugal household (in this case the status which is
closely related to a woman's honour and correct observation of
purdah). Whether these visiting groups could more correctly
be interpreted as part of the women's patron-client networks
(as described by Maher, 1974 for Morocco) is a point that is
open to question and further investigation. Many other relevant
areas of enquiry spring to mind: which women hire other women
as labourers? Which women exchange labour? What class conflicts
exist between women and are they conscious of hierarchy as men
are? How do questions of status affect women's extra-familial
roles? How do women define their status among themselves; what
criteria do they use? These and other questions must be sub-
jected to careful scrutiny in field situations (Zeidenstein,
1976: 12).

Many educators, politicians, and administrators are perturbed
by the fact that so few women are educated, and that relatively
few girls are registered in schools. There needs to be more
comparative and detailed research into attitudes to girls'
education and the structural constraints on their attendance at
different levels of schooling. Why is there so much opposition
to education for girls and how does it correlate with region,
caste, class, religion, and kin structures? Education may be
seen as a disruptive element to traditionally valued marriage
arrangements. In North India it is believed that an educated
woman will be cursed (with barrenness and widowhood) and that
her education will make her dissatisfied with traditional marriage patterns (Jacobson, 1974: 114). Increasing education
of boys may lead to a follow-up emphasis on education for girls,

as Abdullah observed in Bangladesh where people felt that "if you want an educated son-in-law and you do not have an educated girl, you cannot proceed" (1974: 21). On the other hand, people may see education for boys as an investment, while girls' education is merely passed on to a husband. Ahmed points out that there has to be some obvious gain before poor families will educate girls (1976).

In Africa where a bridewealth is often paid to the bride's father at the time of marriage, there may be more motivation to educate daughters since amounts of brideweatlh are directly correlated with the educational achievement of the girl. In Kenya in 1974, I knew of several cases where the father of a University graduate obtained more than £1,500 in bridewealth. Of course, the use of child labour within the household can be a constraint on education for girls. I have already suggested that women's work outside the home may entail increased use of daughters' labour. As quoted above (see p. 79) Arens has shown that in one Bangladesh village, boys' labour was in greater demand than girls', with the result that there are twice as many girls as boys attending primary school (1977: 43).

One fruitful avenue of research to explore would be the question as to why Sri Lanka is the exception to the generally low level of education among women in South Asia. If one could isolate the factors that might be responsible for Sri Lankans' more receptive attitude towards education for girls, it might contribute to our understanding of the whole issue.

Chapter V

Conclusion

In this review I have tried to examine the quality and quantity of research material available on rural women in South Asia, with particular reference to issues and problems related to women's participation in rural development programmes and processes. I have argued that little research has been done, and even less published. Most of the articles and books in this field are lacking in supportive micro-data and rigorous analytical frameworks. After the somewhat superficial review of the issues and problems about which we are best informed, I suggested a selected list of possible avenues of fruitful future research.

It only remains for me to mention briefly the methodological approaches that I would advocate for this suggested research. The kind of problem in question should determine the method employed. For example, the issues raised in connexion with the roles of women and rural development can only be explored by research conducted along anthropological lines. As for problems such as women's perceptions, household decision-making, division of labour and domestic relationships, and assessment of current development programmes, these must be examined by intensive observations over an extended period of time. Lightning visits by teams of research assistants distributing vast numbers of carefully structured questionnaires to random samples of villagers cannot adequately explore questions of social interaction. On the other hand, certain problems are of a type that is better suited to examination by survey methods: factors affecting women's work participation outside the home, as well as those variables relating to women's educational levels or use of family planning. Ideally, hypotheses framed in face-to-face village studies could be tested in large scale, comparative surveys and *vice versa*.

More interdisciplinary research is necessary. The skills of the anthropologist must be allied to those of the economist,

76

demographer, psychologist and historian. Comparaitve analyses
need to be done of existing and future studies, official records,
censuses and other macro-data. Ways and means must also be
found to provide information quickly and accurately to planning
and development agencies both at the stage when programmes are
being designed and later on during stages of implementation to
provide feedback.

A useful device in this context may be the establishment of
centralised registers of national research projects of both
individual scholars and government agencies. This would help
to prevent duplication, would provide some much needed cross-
fertilisation of ideas and would allow scholars interested in
initiating research projects to build on the work done by others
in a systematic manner rather than forever starting from scratch.

One of the constraints on these ambitious proposals is obviously
that of limited resources: time, money and trained personnel.
Several imaginative schemes exist which could perhaps achieve
a research programme on a national scale without inappropriate
expenditure. One has been put forward by T. S. Epstein (1975)
in which she proposes having all social science students spend
part of their University training doing village level research.
This would give them not only firsthand experience of the way
that village people actually live and think (an experience
often sadly lacking in the university-trained, urban, elite
administrators and academics) but would also allow them to suggest and test hypotheses.

Another innovative scheme has been implemented in Sri Lanka by
S. Seneratne. 12 graduate students were given 3 months training
in field methods and subsequently placed in 12 villages, chosen
as representative of the various ethnic, religious and ecological sectors of Sri Lankan society. After they had spent a
period in the field collecting standard ethnographic data,
Seneratne and his team were able to act in a consultancy capa-
city to the Planning Commission. Moreover they were able to
monitor the implementation of current development programmes
and could provide a channel of communication from grass roots
level upwards.

T. S. Epstein, at the University of Sussex, is currently direct-
ing a research project which has exciting possibilities. First
it aims to collect a great deal of solid comparative data on
rural women in five Asian countries. Secondly, it includes an
action programme which will enable the monitoring of technological

and institutional innovations. 12 Asian researchers (10 women
and one husband-wife team) will do village studies in their country of origin where they will collect core data on women and
women's economic roles, as well as other standard anthropological information. At a point in their 20 month stay in the village, the researchers will provide details of existing technology
to Appropriate Technology experts who will be expected to produce designs which subsequently can be tested in field experi-
ments. Village extension workers will also be trained with the
help of the researchers and relevant experts in working with
village women, to encourage them to form associations and be
more self-reliant.

It will be clear to the reader that much of what has been said
in this paper may seem to overemphasise development "from above",
implying that the researcher will direct the results of his
labours to the planner, the government official, the administrator and the implementor. My personal opinion is that in an
ideal world, local populations would have the option to determine the direction(s) that their own lives should take. However,
I am also realistic enough to recognise that in most places
planners and administrators will largely be instrumental in determining the shape and content of many of the social and economic changes taking place. The role of researcher *vis-à-vis*
the planner and administrator raises many difficult, and perhaps
insoluble, problems concerning the way goals and ends are determined. As researchers we do not have the power to take an immediate role in shaping the direction that development processes
take or in mobilising rural people to make their demands felt.
That will be done either by those in power or by impersonal
market forces in most countries (though this is not the only
way that determines which direction is taken). As researchers
we can and must play a part in providing accurate, rigorously
collected and analysed information which is available to both
the implementors and to the people studied, the planners and
the planned for. In addition researchers can perhaps point
out inequalities in the distribution of the "benefits of development" and the sectors which are suffering from relative or abso-
lute disbenefit from development processes or programmes. When
this is done, public opinion (whether on a local, national or
international level) can perhaps be mobilised to redress the
balance. The axe this paper has tried to grind, as I stated
in the beginning, is that women are a disadvantaged sector and
those of us who feel strongly on this matter must speak out
and present the evidence in such a fashion that cannot be con-
tradicted or denied.

Bibliography

Abeywardena, Padmini. January 1977, "Mobilization of Human Resources and Development of Self Reliance — Sri Lanka" in Planning with Rural Women, T. S. Epstein (guest editor), *Les Carnets de l'Enfance*, UNICEF, No. 38.

Abdullah, T. A. 1974, *Village Women as I Saw Them*, The Ford Foundation, Dacca.

*Abdullah, T. A. and Zeidenstein, S. 1978, *Village Women of Bangladesh: Prospects for Change*, Draft of a study done for Employment and Development Department, ILO, Geneva.

Agency for International Development. 1976, "Development of Methodology to Implement Congressional Mandate on the Integration of Women in Development: a Preliminary Study in 3 Countries", A/AID/WID.

Ahmed, Anis. 1975, "The Role of Women in I.R.D.P.", *Integrated Rural Development*, Vol. 1, Dec.: 31-35.

Ahmed, Nizam. 1968, *Peasant, Family and Social Status in East Pakistan*, Ph.D. Thesis, University of Edinburgh.

Ahmed, Shereen. 1967, "Pakistan", *Women in the Modern World*, R. Patai (ed), New York, Free Press.

Akhtar, S. and Arshad, V. 1959, *Village Life in Lahore District A Study of Selected Economic Aspects*, Social Science Research Centre, Lahore, University of Punjab.

Akhtar, S. M. 1963, *Economics of Pakistan*, Vol. I, Lahore, Publishers United.

Alamgir, Susah Fuller. 1977, "Profile of Bangladesh Women's Roles and Status in Bangladesh", Report, USAID, Dacca.

Albreicht, Herbert. 1974, *Living Conditions of Rural Families in Pakistan,* Socio-economic Studies of Rural Development, German Embassy, Islamabad.

Alexander, Paul. 1973, *Risks, Rewards and Uncertainty: Fishermen of Southern Sri Lanka,* Unpublished Ph.D. thesis, Australian National University.

Ali, Azher. 1975, "Rural Development in Bangladesh", Bangladesh Academy for Rural Development.

Ali, Z. A. 1956, "Status of Women in Pakistan", *Pakistan Quarterly,* 6: 46-55.

All Pakistan Women's Association, 1967, *Annual Report,* 1966-67.

Antoun, R. 1968, "On the Modesty of Women in Arab Muslim Villages: A Study in the Accomodation of Traditions", *American Anthropologist,* Vol. 70: 671-697.

Anwar, Seemin and Bilquees, Faiz. 1976, *The Attitudes, Environment and Activities of Rural Women: Case Study of Jhak Sayal,* Research Report No. 98, Pakistan Institute of Development Economics.

Ardener, Shirley, 1975, *Perceiving Women,* London, Malaby Press.

Arens, Jenneke and Van Beurden, Jos. 1977, *Poor Peasants and Women in a Village in Bangladesh,* Amsterdam, Third World Publications.

Asian — Regional Workshop. 1976, "The Role of Women in Contribution to Family Income", Background Paper on Employment of Women in India, Bangkok.

Association of Voluntary Agencies for Rural Development, "Integrated Development Programme of Bolpur Block West Bengal", Al. Kailash Colony, New Delhi.

Azia, Tahmina. 1977, "The Role of Purdah", Paper Produced for Study Seminar 59, "Role of Women in Rural Development", IDS, University of Sussex.

Bagchi, Jasodhara. January 1976, "Killed with Kindness — Review of Indian Women, Towards Equality, Women in Central India", *Economic Political Weekly,* Vol. XI, No. 4: 101-103.

Baig, T. A. 1958, *Women in India*, National Council of Women in India, Ministry of Information, Delhi.

Bailey, F. G. 1957, *Caste and the Economic Frontier*, Manchester, Manchester University Press.

Bangladesh Academy for Rural Development. 1975, *Women's Education and Home Development*, Comilla.

Bean, Lee. 1968, "Utilization of Human Resources: The Case of Women in Pakistan", *International Labour Review*, Vol. 97: 391-410.

Begum, Mahmuda. undated, "Attitude of Pakistan Women Towards Employment", National Institute of Administration, Dacca.

Bertocci, Peter. 1975, "The Position of Women in Rural Bangladesh", Ford Foundation, Bangladesh.

Beteille, Andre. 1975, "Position of Women in Indian Society" in *Indina Women*, D. Jain (ed), New Delhi.

Bhasin, Kamla. 1972, *Position of Women in India*, paper given at a seminar on women in Srinagar.

Bhatnagar, K. S. 1964, *Dikapatura, Village Survey*, Monograph No. 4, Madya Pradesh, Part VI, Census of India, Delhi.

Bhatt, Ela. January 1978, "An Approach to the Rural Poor" in *Role of Rural Women in Development*, ICSSR, Delhi.

Bhatty, Zarina. 1975, "Muslim Women in Uttar Pradesh: Social Mobility and Direction", *Women in Contemporary India*, A. de Souza (ed), Delhi, Manohar.

Bhatty, Zarina. 1976, "Status of Muslim Women and Social Change" in *Indian Women: From Purdah to Modernity*, B. R. Nanda (ed), New Delhi, Vikas.

Billings, Martin and Singh, Arjan. 1970, "Mechanization and the Wheat Revolution: Effects on Female Labour in Punjab", *Economic and Political Weekly*, Vol. 5, No. 52, Dec.: 169-174.

Boserup, Ester. 1970, *Women's Role in Economic Development*, London, Georges Allen & Unwin.

Boserup, Ester. 1975, *Integration of Women in Development:
Why, When, How*, U.N. Development Programme.

Bossen, Laurel. 1975, "Women in Modernizing Societies",
American Ethnologist, Vol. 2, No. 4: 587-601.

Brown, Judigh. 1970, "A note on Division of Labour by Sex",
American Anthropologist, Vol. 72: 1073-78.

Buvinic, Mayra. 1976, *Women in Development: An Annotated
Bibliography*, American Association for the Advancement of
Science, Overseas Development Council.

Carlaw, Raymond. 1971, "Underlying Sources of Agreement and
Communication Between Husband and Wives in Dacca, East Pakistan", *Journal of Marriage and the Family*, Vol. 33:30: 571-83.

Carstairs, Morris. 1975, "Village Women in Rajasthan" in
Indian Women, D Jain (ed), New Delhi.

Castillo, Gelia. undated, "The Women of Ceylon: Some Vital
Statistics", paper.

Castillo, Gelia. 1977, "The Changing Role of Wome in Rural
Societies: A Summary of Trends and Issues", Seminar Report
No. 12, February Agricultural Development Council, Inc.

Chakravorty, Shanti. 1975, "Farm Women Labour: Waste and
Exploitation", *Social Change*, March-June 5:5.

Chambers, Robert and Moris, Jon R. (eds). 1973, *Mwea, an
Irrigated Rice Settlement in Central Kenya*, Weltforum-Verlag,
Afrika-Studien, No. 83, Munich.

Chandna, R. C. 1967, "Female Working Force in Punjab", *Man-
power Journal*, Vol. II, No. 4, January-March: 47-62.

Chatterjee, Afrey. 1975, "Landless Agricultural Women Workers",
Indian Farming, November: 31-33.

Chatterjee, Mary. 1975, *Sweepers of Benares*, unpublished thesis,
Benares University.

Chaudhury, Rifiqul Huda. 1974, "Labour Force Status and Fertility", *Bangladesh Development Studies*, Vol. 2, No. 4:
819-838.

Chawdhari, T. P. S. and Sharma, B. M. 1961, "Female Labour of the Farm Family in Agriculture", *Agricultural Situation in India*, September VI.

Chen, Marty (ed). 1977, *ADAB News*, Special Issue, Vol. IV.

Chen, Marty and Ghuznavi, Ruby. 1977b, *Women in Food-For-Work: The Bangladesh Experience*, Dacca.

Chowdhury, B. K. and Singh, M. N. 1963, *Mavjampur (Bihar) 1955-60, A Study of Socio-economic Change in a Village*, Visva, Bharati.

Commission on Status of Women. 1973, "Status of Rural Women, Especially Agricultural Workers", Report prepared for F.A.O., E/CN6/583/Add 2.

Committee on the Status of Women in India, *Towards Equality*, Government of India, Delhi.

Connell, John. 1973, "Women's Role in Islamic Agriculture", IDS, Internal Working Paper, No. 4, University of Sussex.

Copping, Alice. 1971. "Activities for Education and Training of Women and Girls for Participation in Family and Community Life in Pakistan", UNICEF, E/ICEF/Misc., 163.

Cottam, Christine. 1977, "Women's Secret Banking System in Rajasthan — Towards the Framework for an Analysis", unpublished paper.

Dantwala, M. 1975, "Profile of Poverty and Unemployment in 12 Villages", *Indian Journal of Agricultural Economics*, Vol. XXX, No. 2: 1-7.

Darling, M. L. 1925, *The Punjab of Peasant in Prosperity and Debt*, Oxford University Press.

Dasgupta, Biplab. 1977, *Agrarian Change and New Technology in India*, U.N. Research Inst. Soc. Development, UNRISD/76/C14/GE 76-6281, Geneva.

Dasgupta, Biplab. 1977, "Allocation of Labour Time", Chapter II, *Village Society and Labour Use*, Oxford, Oxford University Press.

Dasgupta, Kalpana. 1976, *Women on the Indian Scene: Annotated Bibliography*, New Delhi, Abhinav Publ.

Dasgupta, Monica. 1975, "From a Closed to an Open System: The Economic Context of Fertility Behaviour in a Green Revolution Village" paper for Population and Rural Poverty Conference, IDS, University of Sussex.

Dasgupta, Monica. 1976, "Ladies First", paper presented to the Fourth World Congress for Rural Sociology, Poland.

Desai, Neera. 1957, *Women in Modern India*, Bombay, Vora & Co.

De Souz, Alfred. 1975, *Women in Contemporary India*, Delhi, Manohar.

Dey, J. M. 1925, *Role of Women in Rural Development in Third World Countries*, M.A. Thesis for Agricultural Extension and Rural Development Centre, University of Reading.

Diamanti, Maria. 1977, "UNICEF and the Participation of Women in Rural Development", paper presented to Study Seminar 59 on The Role of Women in Rural Development, IDS, University of Sussex.

Dixon, Rugh. 1977, *Women's Co-operatives and Rural Development: A Policy Proposal*, Draft report prepared for Resources for the Future Inc., Washington, D.C.

Dodd, P. 1968, "Youth and Women's Emancipation in United Arab Republic", *Middle East Journal*, Vol. 22: 15-72.

Doraiswami, S. April 1975, "Educational Advancement and Socio-Economic Participation of Women in India" in *Design of Educational Programmes for the Promotion of Rural Women*, Conference, International Institute for Adult Literacy Methods.

Dube, Mukul. 1975, "Migration as a Response to Regional Imbalances in Employment Potential: North Saharanpur District", paper presented to a seminar on Cross-cultural Study of Population Growth and Rural Poverty, IDS, University of Sussex.

Dube, S. C. 1955, *Indian Village*, London, Routledge.

Dube, S. C. 1958, *India's Changing Villages: Human Factor in Community Development*, London, Routledge.

Dube, S. C. 1963, "Men's and Women's Roles in India" in
Women in the New Asia, B. Ward (ed), UNESCO.

Economic Commission for Africa. 1975, "The Role of Women in
the Development of the Third World Countries: the African
Experience", UN, M75-1492.

Elgar, Zekeye. 1957, "Punjabi Village" in *Pakistan: Society
and Culture*, S. Maron (ed), New Haven, Connecticut, Human
Relations Area File.

Elgar, Zekeye. 1960, *Punjabi Village in Pakistan*, New York,
Columbia University Press.

Ellickson, Jean. 1975, "Rural Women", *Women for Women*,
Bangladesh.

Elwin, Verrier. 1975, "Tribal Women" in *Indian Women*, D. Jain
(ed), New Delhi.

Epstein, T. Scarlett. 1962, *Economic Development and Social
Change in South India*, Manchester, Manchester University Press.

Epstein, T. Scarlett. 1973, *South India: Yesterday, Today and
Tomorrow*, London, Macmillan.

Epstein, T. Scarlett. 1975, *Rural Social Science Development
and the Role of Women in Rural Development*, Ford Foundation,
Dacca.

Epstein, T. Scarlett (ed). 1977, "Special Issue: Planning
with Rural Women", *Les Carnets de l'Enfance*, Vol. 38, April-
June, UNICEF, Genvea.

Faridi, Tazeen. 1960, *The Changing Role of Women in Pakistan*,
Karachi, Ferozesons.

Farouk, A. and Ali, M. 1975, *The Hardworking Poor: A Survey
on How People Use their Time in Bangladesh*, Bureau of Economic Research, Dacca University.

Firth, Raymond. 1970, "Social Structure and Peasant Economy"
in *Subsistence Agriculture and Economic Development*, C. Wharton
(ed), Chicago, Aldine.

86   Bibliography

F.A.O. 1976, "Requirements and Guidelines for Determining
Women's Economic and Social Contributions to Agricultural and
Rural Development", Home Economics and Social Programme Service.

F.A.O. 1976, "Summary of Discussions of 18th F.A.O. Conference
Related to Home Economics and Social Programme", Home Economics and Social Programmes, Rome, ESH: Misc./76/Z.

Gagdil, D. R. 1964, *Women in the Working Force in India*, Kunda
Datar Memorial Lecture, London, Asia Publishing House.

Gardezi, Dr. Hassan. 1969, *The Dai Study: The Dai (midwife),
a Local Functionnary and Her Role in Family Planning*, West
Pakistan Family Planning Association, Lahore.

Germain, Adrienne. 1975, "Women's Role in Agricultural Development", draft, I/30/75, ADC.

Germain, Adrienne. 1976, *Women's Roles in Bangladesh Development: A Program Assessment*, Ford Foundation, Dacca.

Giele, J. and Smock, A. (eds). 1977, *Women: Roles and Status
in Eight Countries*, New York, John Wiley.

Goody, Jack and Buckley, Joan. 1973, "Inheritance and Women's
Labour in Africa", *Africa*, Vol. 43: 108-121.

Gulati, Leela. 1975a, "Female Work Participation: A Study
in Interstate Difference", *Economic and Political Weekly*,
Vol. X: No. 1-2: 35 January.

Gulati, Leela. 1975b, "Occupational Distribution of Working
Women: an Interstate Comparison", *Economic and Political
Weekly*, Vol. X, No. 43: 169, October.

Gwatkin, Davidson. 1974, *Health and Nutrition in India*, Ford
Foundation, New Delhi.

Haider, Agha. 1960, *Village in an Urban Orbit*, Social Sciences
Research Centre, University of the Punjab Lahore.

Hara, Tadahiko. 1967, *Paribar and Kinship in a Moslem Village
in East Pakistan*, Ph.D. Thesis, Australian National University.

Hardee, J. and Azhar, M. 1975, "Change and Differentials in
Women's Knowledge of, Attitude to and Practice of Family

Planning in Pakistan during the 1960's", *Pakistan Development Review*, Vol. XIV, No. 3: 334-369.

Goonatilake, Hema. 1976, "Social and Political Participation, Tradition, Prejudice, Myth and Reality", *Economic Review*, Sept. 6: 16-17.

Hariss, Barbara. 1977, "Paddy Milling: Problems in Policy and the Choice of Technology" in *The Green Revolution*, B. F. Farmer (ed), London, Billing & Sons Ltd.

Harper, E. 1969, "Fear and the Status of Women", *Southwest Journal of Anthropology*, Vol. 25: 81-95.

Hashimi, Salima. 1968, *Education of Rural Women in West Pakistan*, West Pakistan Agricultural University, Lyallpur.

Haswell, M. R. 1967, *Economics of Development in Village India*, London, Routledge & Kegan Paul.

Hate, Chandrakala. 1969, *Changing Status of Women*, Bombay, Allied Publishers.

Helbock, Lucy. 1975a, *Changing Status of Women in Islamic Pakistan*, USAID, Pakistan.

Helbock, Lucy. 1975b, *Women in Pakistan: An Annotated Bibliography of Materials Dealing with Women's Social and Economic Conditions*, USAID, Pakistan.

Honigmann, John. 1957, "Women in West Pakistan" in *Pakistan: Society and Culture*, S. Maron (ed), Human Relations Area File, New Haven, Connecticut.

Hough, Eleanor. 1966, *Cooperative Movement in India*, Calcutta, Oxford University Press.

Hyder, Qurratulain. 1975, "Muslim Women of India" in *Indian Women*, D. Jain (ed), New Delhi.

Iglitzin, Lynne and Ross, Ruth. 1976, *Women in the World: A Comparative Study*, Santa Barbara, Clio Books.

Ikramullah, S. 1958, "Pakistani Women", *African Women*, Vol. I: June: 89-92.

Indian Cooperative Union. 1976, *Socio-Economic Programme, an Evaluation.* Sponsored by Department of Social Welfare, Government of India.

I.L.O. 1975, "Proposal for an ILO Project on Technological Change and the Condition of Rural Women", World Employment Programme.

I.L.O. 1976, "Employment Growth and Basic Needs", I.L.O. Tripartite World Conference on Employment, Income Distribution and Social Progress and the International Division of Labour.

Islam, Mekerunnesa. 1977, *Food Preparation in Bangladesh,* UNICEF, Dacca Women's Development Programme.

Jacobs, Sue Ellen. 1974, *Women in Perspective: A Guide for Cross-cultural Studies,* Urbana, University of Illinois Press.

Jacobson, D. A. 1970, *Hidden Faces: Hindu and Muslim Purdah in a Central Indian Village,* Ph.D. Thesis, Columbia University.

Jacobson, Doranne. 1974, "Women of North and Central India: Godesses and Wives" in *Many Sisters: Women in Cross Cultural Perspective,* C. Matthiasson (ed), New York, The Free Press.

Jahan, Rounaq. 1974, *Women in Bangladesh,* The Ford Foundation, Dacca.

Jahan, Rounaq. 1975, "Women in Bangladesh", *Women for Women,* Bangladesh.

Jain, Devaki (ed). 1975, *Indian Women,* Publications Division, Ministry of Information and Broadcasting, Government of India.

Jain, Devaki. 1976a, "Measurement of Household Activities in India", Paper for ADC Workshop on Household Studies, Singapore.

Jain, Devaki. 1976b, *Women Workers and Family Planning in the Tea Industry — Report on UPASI Scheme,* Institute of Social Studies, India.

Jayaraman, R. 1975, *Caste Continuities in Ceylon: A Study of the Social Structure of Three Tea Plantations,* Bombay, Popular Prakashan.

Jayardena, Kumari. 1975, "Women of Sri Lanka: Opressed or Emancipated?", *Economic Review*, Vol. 1, No. 3.

Jayaweera, Swarna. 1976, "Formal and Non-Formal Modes of Education Relating to Women with Special Reference to Science, Technical and Vocational Studies in Sri Lanka", Sri Lankan Association for the Advancement of Science, Conference on Scientific and Technological Cooperation among Non-aligned Countries.

Johnson, Orna and Johnson, Allen. 1973, "Male-Female Relations and the Organization of Work in a Machiguenza Community", *American Ethnologist*, Vol. 2 : 2: 634-644.

Kabir, Khushi, Abed, Ayesha and Chen, Marty. 1976, "Rural Women in Bangladesh: Exploding Some Myths", Ford Foundation, Dacca.

Kannangara, Imogen. 1966, "Women's Employment in Ceylon", *International Labour Review*, Vol. 93, No. 2: 117-126.

Karcher, M. 1975, "Report on the Committee on the Status of Women in India".

Karim, Nagmul. 1963, "Changing Patterns of an East Pakistan Family" in *Women in the New Asia*, B. Ward (ed), UNESCO.

Khatun, Saleha and Rani, Gita. 1977, "Bari Based Post Harvest Operations and Livestock Care: Some Observations and Case Studies", Ford Foundation, Dacca.

Korson, Henry. 1975, "Modernization, Social Change and the Family in Pakistan" in *Pakistan in Transition*, W. H. Wriggins, Islamabad University Press.

Lateef, Shahida. undated, "Reform and Response", For a Symposium: Indian Muslims.

Lateef, Shahida. May 1973, "In a Community", paper for a conference on: Status of Women: Symposium on Discriminated Section of Society.

Lateef, Shahida. 1975, "Modernization in India and the Status of Muslim Women", re-working of a paper presented at Harvard University Center of World Religions.

Leach, E. R. 1955, "Polyandry, Inheritance and the Definition
of Marriage", *Man,* Article 199, Vol. 55: 182-186.

Leach, E. R. 1961, *Pul Eliya: A Village in Ceylon,* Cambridge,
Cambridge University Press.

Lewis, Oscar. 1958, *Village Life in Northern India,* New York
City, Vintage Books.

Lindenbaum, Shirley. 1968, "Women and the Left Hand: Social
Status and Symbolism in East Pakistan", *Mankind,* Vol. 6:
537-51.

Lindenbaum, Shirley. 1974, *Social and Economic Status of Women
in Bangladesh,* Ford Foundation, Dacca.

Luschinsky, Mildred Stoop. 1962, *The Life of Women in a
Village of North India: A Study of Role of Status,* Ph. D.
Thesis, Cornell.

Madan, T. N. 1965, *Family and Kinship: Pandits of Rural Kash-
mir,* London, Asia Publishing House.

Madan, T. N. 1975, "Hindu Women at Home" in *Indian Women,*
D. Jain (ed), New Delhi.

Maher, Vanessa. 1974, *Women and Property in Morocco,* Cambridge,
Cambridge University Press.

Maher, Vanessa. 1976, "Kin, Clients and Accomplices: Relations
among Women in Morocco" in *Sexual Divisions and Society,*
Diana Barker (ed), London, Tavistock Press.

Mahmud, Satnam. 1977, "Women and Development", Paper presented
at Seminar on Women and Development, Dacca, Bangladesh.

Mandal, G. C. and Sengupta, S. 1962, *Kashipur, West Bengal
1956-60,* Agro-economic Research Centre, Visva, Bharati.

Mandelbaum, David. 1970, *Society in India,* Vol. I, *Continuity
and Change,* Vol. II, *Change and Continuity,* Berkeley,
University of California Press.

Mankekar, Kamala. 1975, *Women in India: International Women's
Year,* Central Institute of Research & Training in Public
Cooperation, New Delhi.

Martius-von-Harder, Gudrun. 1975, "Participation of Women in Rural Development in 4 Villages: Comilla Kotwali Thana", *Women for Women,* Dacca.

Matthiasson, Carolyn. 1974, *Many Sisters: Women in Cross-cultural Perspective,* New York, The Free Press.

Mayo, Molly. 1976, *Women in their Society: A Selected Bibliography of Pakistan and Other Islamic Countries,* The Ford Foundation, Islamabad.

Mbithi, Philip. 1972, "Issues in Rural Development in Kenya", IDS, Discussion Paper No. 131, University of Nairobi.

McCarthy, Florence. 1967. *Bengalee Village Women: Mediators Between Tradition and Development,* unpublished M.A. thesis, Department of Sociology, Michigan State University, East Lansing.

McCarthy, Florence. 1977, *Report on the Use of Loans by Female Cooperative Members,* Integrated Rural Development Programmes.

McKintosh, Maureen. undated, "The Hardest Work of All: Women and the Process of Industrialization", British Sociological Association.

Mernissi, Fatima. undated, "Muslim Women's Liberation", mimeo paper.

Mernissi, Fatima. 1975, *Beyond the Veil: Male-Female Dynamics in a Modern Muslim Society,* New York, John Wiley & Sons.

Mernissi, Fatima. 1976, "The Moslem World: Women Excluded from Development" in *Women and World Development,* I. Tinker (ed), Overseas Development Council, Washington, D.C.

Mernissi, Fatima. June 1976, "Women's Involvement with Saints and Sanctuaries: A Psychotherapeutic Adaptive Mechanism or a Potential Hotbed of Sedition", Conference: *Women and Development,* Wellesley College.

Michaelson, E. and Goldschmidt, W. 1971, "Female Roles and Male Dominance Among Peasant", *South West Journal of Anthropology,* Vol. 27: 330-350.

Micklewait, Donald and Riegelman, Mary. 1976, *Women in Rural Development*, Boulder, Colorado, Westview Press.

Mitchnik, David. 1972, *Role of Women in Rural Development in Zaire*, Oxfam.

Moore, Michael. undated, "Female Status and Demographic Behaviour", unpublished paper.

Moore, M. P. March 1974, "Some Economic Aspects of Women's Work and Status in Rural Areas of Asia and Africa", IDS, Discussion paper No. 43, University of Sussex.

Mosena, Patricia and Stoeckel, John. August 1971, "The Impact of Desired Family Size upon Family Planning Practices in Rural East Pakistan", *Journal of Marriage and the Family*, Vol. 33: 567-9.

Moss, Manorama. 1976, "The Indian Family — Continuity and Change", UNICEF News, *The Changing Family*, Issue 89/1976/3: 24-28.

Mukherjee, Bishwa Nath. 1974, "The Status of Married Women in Haryana, Tamil Nadu and Meghalaya", *Social Change*, Vol. 4, No. 1: 4-17.

Mukerji, J. 1951, "Status of Indian Women", *International Social Sciences Bulletin*, Vol. 3, No. 4: 793.

Mulla, G. R. 1973, "A Farmer, His Cropping Decisions and Cropping Patterns in India", IDS, working paper No. 2, University of Sussex.

Murphy, Yollanda and Murphy, Robert. 1974, *Women of the Forest*, New York, Columbia University Press.

Nanavati, Manilal. April-June 1961, "A Village in Gujarati", *Indian Journal of Agricultural Economics*, Vol. XVI, No. 2: 1-11.

Nanda, B. R. (ed). 1976, *Indian Women from Purdah to Modernity*, New Delhi, Vikas Publishing.

Narain, Vatsala. 1967, "India" in *Women in the Modern World*, R. Palai (ed), New York, The Free Press.

Nash, June. 1977, "Women in Development: Dependency and Exploitation", *Development and Change*, Vol. 8: 161-182.

Nath, Kamla. 1965, "Women in the New Village", *Economic Weekly*, Bombay, May 15: 813-816.

Nath, Kamla. August 3, 1968, "Women in the Working Force in India", *Economic and Political Weekly*, Vol. III, No. 31: 1205.

Nath, Kamla. May 23, 1970, "Female Work Participation and Economic Development", *Economic and Political Weekly*, Vol. V, No. 21: 846-8.

Nath, Kamla. 1977, "Work Participation and Social Change among Rural Women: A Case Study in Eastern Rajasthan, India", unpublished paper.

National Board of Bangladesh Women's Rehabilitation Programme. 1974, *Women's Work: 18 February 1972-June 1974*, Dacca.

Nelson, Cynthia and Olesen, Virginia. 1977, "Veil of Illusion: A Critique of the Concept of Equality in Western Feminist Thought", *Catalyst*, No. 10-11, Summer: 8-36.

Nelson, Nici. forthcoming, "'Women Must Help Each Other': the Operation of Personal Networks among Buzaa Beer Brewers in a Mathare Valley, Kenya" in *Women Divided, Women United*, P. Caplan and J. Bujra (eds), London, Tavistock.

Nelson, Nici. forthcoming summer 1978, "Female Centred Families: Changing Patters of Marraige and Family Among Buzaa Brewers of Mathare Valley", *African Urban Notes*, special issue on E. Africa.

Nowiki, Jozef. 1973, *Some Contradictions and Barriers of Development in Bangladesh*, The Ford Foundation, Dacca.

O'Kelly, Elizabeth. 1977, *Simple Rural Technologies for Rural Women in Bangladesh*, UNICEF, Dacca Women's Development Programme.

Obeysekere, Gananath. 1963, "Pregnancy Cravings in Relation to Social Structure and Personality in a Sinhalese Village", *American Anthropology*, LXV: 2: 326.

Obeysekere, Gananath. 1967, *Land Tenure in Village Ceylon*, Cambridge, Cambridge University Press.

Olin, Ulla. 1976a, "Case for Women as Co-Managers: the Family as a General Model of Human Social Organization" in *Women and World Development*, I. Tinker (ed), New York, Traeger Publishers.

Olin, Ulla. 1967b, "Women's Demand for Family Planning Services", World Bank Population Mission to India.

Olin, Ulla. 1977, "Integration of Women in Development Programme Guidelines, a Draft".

Omer, Salma. 1961, "Women's work in C.D.A. Community Development — Its Significance and Impediments", *Community Development Bulletin*, 4: Sept: 133-138.

Omvedt, Gail. 1975, "Caste, Class and Women's Liberation in India", *Bulletin of Concerned Asian Scholars*, Special Issue: Asian Women, Vol. 7, No. 1: 41-48.

Omvedt, Gail. 1977, "Women and Rural Revolt in India", *South Asia Papers*, Vol. 1, No. 4-5, May.

Organization for Cooperation and Development. 1976, "Integrated Approach to Improving the Status of Young Women in Developing Countries", Background paper for a working group.

Pakistan Sociological Association. 1968, *Pakistan Sociological Perspective*, Pakistan.

Pala, Achola. December 1976, *African Women in Rural Development: Research Trends and Priorities*, Overseas Liaison Committee, American Council on Education, OLC paper; No. 12.

Palmer, Ingrid. 1975, "Women in Rural Development", unpublished paper.

Palmer, Ingrid. 1977, "Rural Women and the Basic Needs Approach to Development", *International Labour Review*, Vol. 115, No. 2: 97-107.

Pande, J. K. 1949-50, *Agricultural Economy Village Chitra Agra District*, Government of Uttar Pradesh (Allahabad), Department of Economic Statistics.

Papanek, Hanna. 1971, "Purdah in Pakistan: Seclusion in Modern
Occupations for Women", *Journal of Marriage and the Family*,
Vol. 33, No. 3: 517-30.

Papanek, Hanna. 1973, "Purdah: Separate Worlds and Symbolic
Shelters", *Comparative Studies in Society and History*,
Vol. 15, No. 3: 283-325.

Papanek, Hanna. 1975, "The Work of Women: Post Script from
Mexico City", *Signs: Journal of Women in Culture and Society*,
Autumn, Vol. 1, No. 1: 215-26.

Papanek, Hanna. 1975, "Women in South and South East Asia:
Issues and Research", *Signs: Journal of Women in Culture and
Society*, Vol. 1, No. 1: 193-212.

Pastner, Carol. 1971, *Sexual Dichotomization in Society and
Culture: Women of Panjgur, Baluchistan*, Ph.D. Thesis,
Brandeis.

Pastner, Carol. 1974, "Accomodations to Purdah: The Female
Perspective", *Journal of Marriage and the Family*, Vol. 136,
No. 2: 408-413.

Patai, R. 1967, *Women in the Modern World*, New York, The Free
Press.

Patel, A. and Athonio, Q. 1973, *Farmers Wives in Agricultural
Development: The Nigerian Case*, XV International Congress
of Agricultural Economists: The Nigerian Case, Sao Paulo.

Patnaik, G. N. 1964, *Gundurigora, Orissa: Report on Re-survey
of a Village: 1958-64*, Agro-economic Research Centre, Visva,
Bharati.

Patnaik, G. N. 1966, *A Report on Re-survey of a Village in
Orissa: 1954-66*, Agro-economic Research Centre, Visva,
Bharati.

Patnaik, G. N. 1967, *Kasoti: Orissa*, Agro-economic Research
Centre, Visva, Bharati.

Perera, Lakshmi. August 1977, *Women and Development: Research
Design*, Colombo, Leiden.

Pieris, Ralph. 1956, *Sinhalese Social Organization*, Colombo, Ceylon University Press Board.

Pieris, Ralph. 1962, "Cultural Matrix of Development", *Ceylon Journal of Historical and Social Studies*, Vol. 5, No. 1, 2: 18-34.

Pieris, Ralph. 1965, "Effects of Technological Development on Population of Gal Oya Valley", *Ceylon Journal of Historical and Social Studies*, Vol. 8, No. 1, 2: 163-191.

Presvelou, C. 1975, "The Invisible Woman", *Ceres*, F.A.O, Vol. 8, No. 2: 50-53.

Rahman, Jowsham. 1975, *Population Planning through Mother's Clubs*, *Annual Report*, Department of Social Welfare, Bangladesh.

Rai, S. 1975, "Education of our Rural Women Folk", *Education Quaterly*, Vol. XXVII, No. 2: 18-19.

Ramachandran, Padma. 1977, "Role of Women in Rural Development", paper given at study seminar 59, The Role of Women in Rural Development, IDS, University of Sussex.

Ranasinghe, W. 1977, A Bibliography of Socio-economic Studies in the Agrarian Sector of Sri Lanka, Agrarian Research and Training Institute, Colombo.

Reddy, Narasimha. June 7, 1975, "Female Work Participation: a Study of Inter-state Differences", *Economic and Political Weekly*, Vol. X, No. 23: 902-3.

Reining, Patricia. 1977, *Village Women, their Changing Lives and Fertility: Studies in Kenya, Mexico, the Phillipines*, American Association for the Advancement of Science, Washington, D.C.

Reiter, Rayna. 1975, *Toward an Anthropology of Women*, New York & London, Monthly Review Press.

Research Unit on Women's Studies, S.N.D.T. 1975, *Women in India*, Bombay, Women's University.

Reynolds, Richard. 1965, *Prospects for Population Control in Pakistan*, The Ford Foundation, New Delhi.

Rogers, Barbara. 1977, "Women should not be Afterthoughts", *Development Forum*, Jan-Feb: 8.

Rogers, Susan. 1975, "Female Forms of Power and the Myth of Male Dominance in Peasant Societies", *American Ethnology*, Special Issue on Sex Roles in Cross-cultural Perspective, Vol. 2, No. 4: 727-56.

Rosaldo, Michelle. 1974, "Women, Culture and Society: a Theoretical Overview" in *Women, Culture and Society*, M. Rosaldo and L. Lamphere (eds), California, Stanford University Press.

Rosen, George. 1975, *Peasant Society in a Changing Economy: Comparative Development in South East Asia and India*, Urbana, University of Illinois.

Roy, M. 1975, *Bengali Women*, Chicago, University of Chicago Press.

Rubin, Gayle. 1975, "The Traffic in Women: Notes of the Political Economy of Sex" in *Towards an Antrhopology of Women*, R. Reiter (ed), new York, Monthly Review Press.

Ryan, D. 1955, "Agricultural System fo a Ceylon Jungle Village", *Eastern Anthropology*, No. 8: 151-160.

Ryan, D. 1956, *The Sinhalese Village*, University of Maimu.

Sadiq, Malik. 1975, "Participation of Rural Women in Integrated Rural Development Programme in Pakistan", paper presented for seminar on Role and Status of Women in Pakistan, Pakistan Administrative Staff College, Lahore, Oct 29-31.

Saeed, Kishwar. 1966, *Rural Women's Participation in Farm Operations*, West Pakistan Agricultural University.

Saeed, S. A. December 1968, "Problems of Female Education in Rural Areas", *The Pakistan Review*, Vol. XVI, No. 12: 23-5.

Sanday, Peggy. 1974, "Female Status in the Public Domain" in *Women, Culture and Society*, M. Rosaldo and L. Lamphere (eds), Stanford University Press, California.

Sattar, Ellen. 1974, *Women in Bangladesh*, The Ford Foundation, Dacca.

Sattar, Ellen. 1975, "Village Women's Work" in *Women for Women*, Bangladesh.

Schendel, Willem. 1976, *Bangladesh*, University of Amsterdam, Voor Publikatie, No. 10.

Schofield, Susan. 1974, "The Seasonal Factors Affecting Nutrition in Different Age Groups", *The Journal of Development Studies*, Vol. II, No. 1: 22-40.

Schoustra-Van-Beukering, E. J. 1975, "Sketch of the Daily Life of a Bengali Village Woman", *Plural Societies*, Vol. VI, No. 4.

Seers, Dudley, 1974, *Meaning of Development*, IDS, Communication Series, No. 44.

Sengupta, Padmani. 1960, *Women Workers of India*, New Delhi, Asia Publishing House.

Sengupta, Padmani. 1964, *Women in India*, Ministry of External Affairs, New Delhi.

Sengupta, Padmani. 1974, *The Story of Indian Women*, New Delhi, Indian Book Co.

Sengupta, Sankar. 1970, *A Study of Women in Bengal*, Calcutta. Indian Publishing.

Sengupta, Sunil. 1957, *Four Villages of West Bengal 1956-7*, Agro-economic Research Center, Visva, Bharati.

Sengupta, Sunil. 1964, *Summary Reports on Socio-economic Surveys: 8 villages of Bihar, 5 villages of Orissa*, Vol. II, Agro-economic Research Centre, Visva Bharati.

Shah, Nasra. 1975, "Female Labour Force Participation and Fertility Desires in Pakistan", *Pakistan Development Review*, Vol. XIV, No. 2: 185-205.

Shah, Nasra. 1977, "Fertility of Workers vs. Non-workers Women in Pakistan, 1973", Paper presented to Seminar on Women in Development, Dacca, Bangladesh.

Shaukat-Ali, Parveen. 1975, *The Women on the Third World: a Comprehensive Bibliography with an Introductory Essay*, Lahore, Progressive Publishers.

Singer, Hans. 1973, "The Development Outlook for Poor Countries: Technology is the Key", *Challenge*, May June.

Singh, Andrea Menefee. October-December 1975, "The Study of Women in India: Some Problems in Methodology" in *Women in Contemporary India*, A. de Souza (ed), Delhi, Mamohas.

Siniwardene, S. 1958, "Pattern of Social Life in Village of Kotikapola", *Journal of Historical and Social Studies*, Vol. I, No. 2: 163-179.

Siniwardene, S. 1963, "The Life of Ceylon Women" in *Women in the New Asia*, B. Ward (ed), UNESCO.

Siniwardene, S. 1974, "Educational Achievements and Prospects of Employment of Women in Sri Lanka", Seminar paper, Investment in Women, Cambridge.

Slocum, A. 1959, *Village Life in Lahore District: A Study of Selected Sociological Aspects*, Social Science Research Centre, University of the Punjab, Lahore.

Smithells, Janice. 1972, *Agricultural Extension Work among Rural Women*, University of Reading, Agricultural Extension and Rural Development Centre.

Smock, Audrey. 1977, "Bangladesh: A Struggle with Tradition and Poverty" in *Women: Roles and Status in Eight Countries*, J. Giele and A. Smock (eds), New York, John Wiley & Sons.

Sridharan, Sumi. 1975, "In Chatera", *Indian Farming*, November pp. 43-46.

Srinivas, M. N. undated paper, "Research Problems Concerning Status of Women in India".

Srinivas, M. N. November 1976a, "Changing Position of Indian Women", Huxley Memorial Lecture, London School of Economics.

Srinivas, M. N. 1976b, *The Remembered Village*, Berkeley, University of California.

Stevens, R. D. and Bertocci, P. 1976, *Rural Development in Bangladesh and Pakistan*, Hawaii, East West Book Center.

Stoeckel, J. and Choudhury, K. M. A. 1972, "Seasonal Variations in Births in Rural East Pakistan", *Journal of Bisocial Science,* Vol. IV: 107-116.

Stokes, Olivia. 1975, "Women of Rural Bihar" in *Indina Women,* Devaki Jain (ed), New Delhi.

Stoler, Ann. 1975, "Land Labour and Female Autonomy in a Javanese Village", paper produced for the Anthropology Department, Columbia University.

Strathern, Marilyn. 1972, *Women in Between, Female roles in a male world:* Mount Hagen, New Guinea, London and New York, Seminar Press.

Subcommittee on Women in Development. 1975, "Criteria for Evaluation of Development Projects Involving Women", Committee on Development Assistance, American Council of Voluntary Agencies.

Sweeney, C. 1976, "Despised and Rejected, the Most Miserable Women on Earth", *Guardian,* Thursday, September 16.

Szalai, Alexander. 1975, "Women's Time: Women in the Light of Contemporary Time-Budget Research", *Futures,* Vol. 7, No. 5: 385-99.

Thamarajakshi, R. undated circa 1975-76, "Women in Indian Agriculture", unpublished paper.

Tinker, I. October-December 1976, "Development and the Disintegration of the Family", *Assignment Children,* No. 36: 29-37.

Tinker, I. 1976a, "The Adverse Impact of Development on Women" in *Women and World Development,* I. Tinker, M. Bo Bramsen and M. Buvinić (eds), Washington, D.C., Overseas Development Council.

Tinker, I. 1976b, "Introduction", *Women and World Development,* I. Tinker, M. Bo Bramsen and M. Buvinić (eds), Washington, D.C., Overseas Development Council.

Tobias, George. 1970, *Human Resources Development and Utilization in the 1970's,* New Delhi, The Ford Foundation.

Tray, Dennis. 1977, "Household Studies Workshop", Seminar Report No. 13, May, Agricultural Development Council, Inc.

Trivedi, Nivedita. 1976, "Marriage Arrangements and the Status of Women", *Modernization, Stagnation and Steady Decline: Sociological Contributions on Social Change in South Gujarat, India,* Centre for Comparative Social-Economic Studies, University of Utrecht, Holland.

UNICEF. 1977, *Report of a Feasibility Survey of Productive/ Income Generating Activities for Women in Bangladesh,* Dacca.

U.N. Research Institute for Social Development. 1977a, "Monitoring Changes in the Condition of Women: a Research Proposal", UNRISD/77/C.2, Geneva.

U.N. Research Institute for Social Development. 1977b, "Monitoring Changes in the Condition of Women: Design for Phase Two", UNRISD/77/C.24, Geneva.

Visva-Bharati University. 1959, "Sihorwa-Bihar, 1958-9", Agro-economic Research Centre, no author.

Vogel, Eliane. 1975, "Some Suggestions for the Advancement of Working Women", *International Labour Review,* Vol. 112, No. 1: 29-43.

Von Fellenberg, Theodor. 1965, "Social Relations in a Sinhalese Village", *Ceylon Journal of Historical and Social Studies,* Vol. 8, No. 1-2: 119-129.

Vreede de Stuers, Cora. 1960, *The Indonesian Woman: Struggle and Achievements,* Gravenhage, Mouton & Co.

Vreede de Stuers, Cora. 1968, *Purda, a Study of Moslem Women's Life in North India,* Studies of Developing Countries, No. 8.

Wallman, S. 1976, "Difference, Differentiation, Discrimination", *New Community,* Journal of Community Relations Commission, Vol. 5 (1-2), 1: 14.

Weisblat, A. M. October 1975, "Role of Rural Women in Development", a seminar report, New York, The Agricultural Development Council.

Wilbur, Donald. 1964, *Pakistan, Its People, Its Society, Its Culture,* New Haven, Conneticut, Human Relation Area File.

Wiser, William and Charlotte. 1963, *Behind Mud Walls,* Berkeley. University of California Press.

Wolf, Margery. 1972, *Women and the Family in Rural Taiwan,* California, Stanford University Press.

Women for Women Research and STudy Group. 1975, *Women for Women,* Dacca, University Press Ltd.

Women's Research and Training Centre, United Nations Economic Commission for Africa. 1975, "Women and National Development in African Countries", *African Studies review,* Vol. XVIII, No. 3: 47-70.

Worsley, P. M. (ed). 1971, *Two Blades of Grass,* Manchester, Manchester University Press.

Yalman, Nur. 1963, "On the Purity of Women in the Castes of Ceylon and Malabar", Journal of the Royal Anthropological Institute.

Yalman, Nur. 1967, *Under the Bo Tree: Studies in Caste, Kinship and Marriage in the Interior of Ceylon,* Berkeley, University of California.

Youssef, Nadia. 1974, *Women and Agricultural Production in Muslim Societies,* Princeton, Princeton University Press.

Youssef, Nadia. 1974, *Women and Work in Developing Societies,* Berkeley, Institute of International Studies University of California.

Youssef, Nadia. 1976, "Women in the Muslim World" in *Women in the World: A Comparative Study,* New York, Clio Books.

Zeidenstein, Sondra and Laura. 1973, "Observations on the Status of Women in Bangladesh", The Ford Foundation, Dacca.

Zeidenstein, Sondra. 1975, "Socio-economic Implications of HYV Rice Production on Rural Women of Bangladesh", Dacca, mimeo paper.

Zeidenstien, Sondra. 1976, *Report on First Two Years of the
I.R.D.P. Pilot Project on Population Planning and Rural Women's
Cooperatives*, Unpublished paper.

GOVERNMENT PUBLICATIONS AND SYMPOSIA

Agricultural Development Council. 1974, "Prospects for Growth
in Rural Societies with or without Active Participation of
Women", Princeton, N.J.

Pakistan Statistical Division Ministry of Finance Planning and
Economic Development, June 9, 1973 *Labour Force Survey 1971-1972*.
Karachi.

Role and Status of Women in Pakistan, October 1975, International
Women's Year Seminar, Pakistan Administrative Staff College,
Lahore.

Bangladesh Economic Research Bureau. *Statistical Abstract of
Bangladesh*. 1972, Society and Commerce Publications.

Statistical Digest of Bangladesh. 1972, Dacca.

JOURNALS

Economic Revies. Sept. 1976, "Women and Development", Sri
Lanka.

Indian Farmer. Nov. 1975, "Women", India.

Indian Journals of Agricultural Economis. July 1978, "Dairy
Development and Bouine Economy", Vol. XXX, No. 3: 82-171.

Indian Worker. Aug. 19, 1974, "Women's Role in Rural Development", Vol. XXII: 67-68.

Pakistan Horizon 1975 "Women in Tomorrow's Pakistan: Symposium
at Pakistan Institute of International Affairs, Karachi",.
Vol XXVIII, No 2.

Appendix

Schoustra-van-Beukering (1975)

Women's Work in a Bangladesh Village

	Daily task/activity (t) (a)	Radius of action	Equipment	Time
1 a	Get up, go to latrine, wash face, hands, legs, mouth, go to prayer	house and compound	bodna, water, piece of coal (toothpaste), gamcha (towel), napkin towel	15 minutes
2 t	Fold up bed, put lamp away	in house, sometimes on veranda	mat katha (rags), pillow	10 minutes
3 t	Wash dishes (of last night's dinner)	in compound, near the well in the pond	thala (plate), bati (cup), glass, kari (frying pan), dekchi (small cauldron), gamla (dish), spoons with: ashes and grass and skin of coconut	1 hour
4 t	Cook breakfast	kitchen	fire, stove, fire-wood, water, rice (bread), grinding wheat	1-2 hours
5 t	Clean the children	near the well on the compound	piece of coal, water, towel	about 15 minutes
6 a	Have breakfast with family	kitchen	bread (handmade) or rice with gur or curry	15 minutes-1 hour
7 t	Wash breakfast dishes	in compound, near the well in the pond	thala (plate), glass and one serving spoon	15 minutes

8 t	Sweep house, kitchen, compound	in compound, near the well in the pond	broom	1½ hours
9 t	Bring water from pond or well for cooking and washing, from tubewell for human consumption	pond outside compound or well inside or tubewell	brass pots, mud pots, aluminium bucket	depending on distance 15 minutes-1 hour
10 t	Wash clothes of the whole family	pond or well	clothes: pants, pyjamas, frock saree, lungi, with or without soap or soda	1-2 hours
11 t	Cook lunch	kitchen	cauldron, spoon, frying pan, kathi (small stick to stir), khunti, (spud paddle), orong (spoon from coconut) malsha (small pot round earthenpot), chula (stove), firewood.	2-3 hours
12 a	Take daily bath, bathe children	in compound with well-water or in pond	big pot, small mug (cup), soap or no soap	15 minutes-1½ hours
13 a	Have lunch	kitchen or veranda	thala, glass, spoon, pin (wooden stool), rice, dal, fish, potato, brinjil, bean, tomato	about 1 hour (it is about 1-3 o'clock)
14 a	Take betelnut or panleaf	kitchen or veranda	pan, chupan, chun, one brass plate, one dish, betelnut crackers (jati), some tins for keeping lime, khair (red-making material)	5 minutes

15 a	Take rest	on veranda or in house	mat, pillow, katha	1-1½ hours
16 t	Take laundry from line	compound	clothes, katha	5 minutes
17 t	Sweep house and compound	compound	broom	1½ hours
18 t	Wash the children	near the well on compound	piece of coal, water, towel	about 15 minutes
19 t	Clean lamp and fill it	in kitchen	hurricane lamp or kupi (oil-lamp), matches, kerosine oil	5 minutes
20 t	Cook dinner	kitchen	rice, vegetables, leftovers from lunch curry	1-2 hours
21 a	Eat dinner	kitchen	items 13 and 20	about 1 hour
22 t	Make bed	in house	bedding	15 minutes

Inter-seasonal Activities (November-February)

	Daily task	Radius of action	Equipment	Time
1	Hang katha (bedding)	compound outside	bamboo line, rope	7-8 minutes
2	Boil rosh	compound, in outside chula	big flat tin pan, orong (coconut made spoon)	1-3 hours morning and afternoon
3	Roast paddy	compound, in outside chula	flat or round pan	1-3 hours several days

4	Dry paddy	compound on mat	mat, basket	many days
5	Husk the dried roasted paddy	compound	dheki (paddyhusk)	many hours several days
6	Clean paddy	compound	winnowing fan, basket	many hours several days
7	Store paddy	compound or in house	in big mud pot, or in outside store	several hours
8	Prepare several kinds of cake	kitchen	powder rice, grinding rice, milk gur, cauldron, etc.	about 1 hour
9	Make lime (1) collect shells (2) clean shells (3) burn shells (4) put in water (5) dry (6) store	compound	shells, bucket, cowdung, pot for storing	several days
10	Collect firewood	around in the village, in the bush	sticks, cowdung, skin of paddy water	about 30

Household Tasks Which Occur Regularly (not daily)

	Daily task	Radius of action	Equipment	Time
1	Plastering floor every 5 to 10 days	house, compound, kitchen, veranda	pot, water, mud, cowdung, piece of cloth	1-3 hours
2	Wash clothes	pond outside compound, well inside compound	soda, soap, basket to hold the clothes	1-1½ hours

3	Make vegetable garden	compound (outer one)	spade, digging hoe, bucket	1-1½ hours

Rainy Season

Daily task	Radius of action	Equipment	Time
More sewing	on veranda or in the house	needle, thread, cloth	depends — mainly in afternoon